Social Town Citizens
Discover
82
New Unthinkables
for Superflex® to Outsmart!

Introducing Superflex's

VERY COOL FIVE-STEP POWER PLAN

and the

Thinkables

Social Thinking Publishing, San Jose, California

www.socialthinking.com

**Social Town Citizens Discover
82 New Unthinkables for Superflex to Outsmart!**
Introducing Superflex's Very Cool Five-Step Power Plan
and the Thinkables

Edited and Expanded upon by Stephanie Madrigal, MA, CCC-SLP,
Michelle Garcia Winner, MA, CCC-SLP and Pamela Crooke, PhD

Library of Congress Control Number: 2012942336

ISBN: 978-0-9792922-2-4
012015

Cover image: iStockphoto/Sigal Suhler Moran

Social Thinking Publishing
3031 Tisch Way, Suite 800
San Jose, CA 95128
Phone: (877) 464-9278
Fax: (408) 557-8594

This book is printed and bound in Tennessee by Mighty Color Printing.

Books may be ordered online at www.socialthinking.com.

Advance Praise **Hetler**

for

Social Town Citizens Discover 82 New Unthinkables for Superflex to Outsmart!

"It comes as no surprise that Michelle and Stephanie have produced yet another invaluable resource tool for those of us in the Social Thinking trenches! My students already love Superflex and to have more Superflex strategies and Unthinkables to defeat, created by the community, is beyond exciting! We use this program not only with our ASD kids but have also incorporated Superflex into our K-6 social skills curriculum. This new resource is an excellent extension of the Superflex family! We are forever fans!"

–Dr. Lori Liguori, NCSP, School Psychologist, Stonington, CT

"The Five-Step Power Plan gives us a 'social formula' that can be applied to any situation to help defeat anyone's Unthinkables. The new team of Thinkables brings to life all the skills needed to be social thinkers. Just like focusing on the Unthinkable that needs to be defeated, we can focus on the Thinkable that will help defeat it!"

–Maria Sasaki Reilly, BCBA

"I work with elementary school students who have attention and social deficits. My students have trouble sitting quietly and listening to a lesson but when I introduced your superheroes I had them hooked! Superflex and the Unthinkables are like comic books to them. Your characters make difficult social concepts accessible to my students. Instead of fighting for their attention they can't wait to hear another story.

Social thinking is difficult for the best of us but your new Five-Step Power Plan is just what is needed to break down complex social behaviors into teachable components. And the new Thinkables will give our students concrete examples of the pro-social behaviors that we want them to display. We can emphasize teaching the desired skill and offer alternatives to undesirable behaviors."

–Elaine Omanoff, School Psychologist, Union School District, San Jose, CA

"Superflex once again saves the day with his easy to implement Very Cool Five-Step Power Plan. My students benefit from the new Unthinkables and this powerful program. It's 'over the top' engaging and readily useable. Even better, the new Thinkables give more support to those constantly struggling to make good choices and learning how their thinking and behavior impacts themselves and others. My goal is to infuse Superflex thinking and strategies in everyday interactions in my classroom."

– Cindy Loper, SDC Teacher, Alta Vista Elementary School-Union School District

"*Social Town Citizens Discover 82 New Unthinkables...* is exactly what our students needed to power up their superflexible thinking! The new student-created Unthinkables combined with Superflex's Very Cool Five-Step Power Plan is a winning strategy to inspire and energize Social Thinking across Superflex Nation!"

– Katy Shamitz, Social Educator, Founder & Director of Skills for Living

Heffer

Dedicated to the 500 outstanding citizens of Social Town who submitted proposals for this book and to the hundreds more who send their ideas to our office. They teach and inspire us daily – and their creativity warms our brain sensors! We're proud of our Social Town community and all they teach us.

-The Social Town Mayor Stephanie Madrigal and Town Councilwoman Michelle Garcia Winner

Contents

CHAPTER 4: PRESENTING 82 NEW UNTHINKABLES.........................37

CONTENTS

CONTENTS

CONTENTS

CHAPTER 1
Introduction

How Superflex Came to Be

Superflex, a Social Thinking superhero, is a concept developed out of desperation by therapist Stephanie Madrigal who was struggling, as all therapists do at times, with capturing the attention of and motivating one of her students. The ironic part about trying to teach this student to use flexible thinking and change his behavior was that Stephanie had to call on her own flexibility and change her approach. This wasn't something she was used to doing. She had had much success coming up with activities and games that excited and engaged other students to explore social thinking and being a part of a group. But this student was different.

Stephanie knew she was in for a challenge with this student when he spent the first session under the table refusing to work with her. During the second session, he didn't go under the table but rather left the room when the smallest demand was placed on him. Feeling helpless, Stephanie chose to think about the session from the student's perspective and what he'd want to be doing or talking about with her. That was easy given his obsession with superheroes. So she went to work.

When he arrived for his next session, a superhero was drawn on the board in the therapy room with the name "Superflex" written above. Before Stephanie could even introduce the character, the student asked several questions about this hero. Stephanie proudly explained that Superflex was an imaginary superhero who is in all of our brains to guide our thinking and help us become the best social thinkers we could be. She remembers noticing that this was the first time the student had looked at her. She proceeded to describe how Superflex had a nemesis like any other superhero. This nemesis named Rock Brain wanted to constantly challenge people's Superflex thinking so they insist on only doing things one way, their way. Rock Brain made people

become stuck on their ideas and their plans. For the remainder of that year, Stephanie and this student explored his brain, his thinking, and the superflexible powers he possessed.

That summer, her group of colleagues began to explore the idea of incorporating more characters that helped identify those unexpected behaviors they constantly talked about with their students as challenging their thinking. The following Team of Unthinkables was born:

- Rock Brain, who makes people stuck on their ideas
- Glassman, who gets people to have huge reactions
- D.O.F., The Destroyer of Fun, who makes people overly competitive
- Mean Jean, who gets people to act mean and bossy
- One-Sided Sid, who gets people to only talk about themselves
- Energy Hare-y, who gives people too much energy
- Body Snatcher, who moves people's bodies away from the group
- Grump Grumpaniny, who puts people in grumpy moods
- Un-Wonderer, who doesn't like people to show interest in others (social wondering)
- Worry Wall, who makes people jump off topic
- WasFunnyOnce, who gets people to use humor at the wrong time
- Space Invader, who gets people to invade others' personal space
- Brain Eater, who gets people distracted
- Topic Twistermeister, who gets people to say things off topic

This original Team of Unthinkables is described in greater detail in chapter 3 of this book.

Citizens of Social Town Respond

In 2008, both *Superflex®…A Superhero Social Thinking Curriculum* and the first Superflex comic book about Rock Brain were released. They quickly became popular among children and teachers. Four years and two more comic books later, people around the country and the world continue to embrace the Superflex curriculum and its cast of characters to assist in teaching Social Thinking. Our very own Social Town City Hall has been inundated with inspiring letters, emails, and phone calls from citizens sharing their great Superflex ideas, accomplishments, and excitement. Children in groups, along with their support teams, have created Superflex movies, commercials, plays, drawings, comic books, and Unthinkable and Superflex costumes and puppets. Schools have also found creative ways to infuse the curriculum and vocabulary into mainstream classes with

CHAPTER 1 © 2012 SOCIAL THINKING PUBLISHING

younger students and use them throughout the school day to encourage social thinking.

Our biggest response at Social Town City Hall has come from students who have been eager to share their own Unthinkable creations along with stories of how their new Unthinkable helped them think more about a specific behavior and motivated them to develop strategies to defeat the Unthinkable. Several teams also came up with Thinkable characters that complement the Unthinkable team. The Thinkables were created to provide a way to manage students' behavior by focusing on expected behaviors.

Superflex and the Mayor and other officials of Social Town were so impressed and excited by the enthusiasm and love for Superflex that they wanted to provide a way to honor the community's desire to share their ideas with others. The idea for this book was born.

We announced the opportunity for kids, teachers, and parents to submit applications that named their own Unthinkable or Thinkable along with an explanation of the character's powers and the Superflex strategies they would use to defeat the Unthinkable. Submissions came from children, therapists, and teachers, some of whom encouraged whole classes to create characters. We received an overwhelming 500 submissions and selected 96 characters to represent the newest additions to the Unthinkables and Thinkables team. We were really impressed and grateful for all the amazing creativity.

Most authors included their own artwork with their submissions. We produced illustrations for those who didn't submit them. Each author is recognized in chapter 6 along with biographical information and any words of wisdom they shared about their Unthinkable or Thinkable. Our Social Town governmental bodies carefully reviewed and edited the materials for each new character. This was done to ensure a consistent teaching direction that ties in with the newly developed powers of Superflex described next.

Superflex Reveals His Hidden Powers

Superflex and the Team of Unthinkables have been well received by kids, parents, counselors, and teachers around the world. Adults have even asked us to create a similar program to encourage their own social learning. We've enjoyed watching the community's enthusiasm and creativity emerge around this teaching concept. Citizens have also

Note:
This book builds on the existing Superflex books and core Social Thinking Vocabulary as presented in *You Are a Social Detective!*, *Superflex®...A Superhero Social Thinking Curriculum*, and *Think Social! A Social Thinking Curriculum for School-Age Students*. It's assumed that readers of this book are already familiar with those concepts and vocabulary terms. Please see the Bibliography if you need an introduction to or review of Superflex and Social Thinking before using this book.

let us know that the Superflex curriculum has been a little problematic for some students, at times causing resistance, unexpected behaviors, or increased rigid thinking. For this group, Superflex is probably not the best option. But for the many others, we've continued to review and improve our Superflex materials. We appreciate all the positive and constructive feedback that has helped us to do this.

As part of this ongoing process of evolving our thinking and teaching about Superflex, we recognized that our book, *You Are a Social Detective!* offers a critical link for helping students, teachers, and parents learn the value of **observing** a situation to understand what's expected to say or do to use a Superflex strategy. A number of counselors have suggested we teach students to **stop and think** to be able to figure out which of many possible strategies they might use. From our own teaching and suggestions from others, we realized how important it is for each child to be able to **describe and decide** which Unthinkable that student is working on as well as **think** about the hidden rules and **coach** themselves through the process. In fact, we think these five areas are so important that the Town Council of Social Town (Madrigal, Winner, and Crooke) met and voted to reveal these critical powers to you and your students in this book as well as in all future materials we develop based on Superflex.

This means that you — the teacher, other professional, or parent — will have the opportunity to explicitly teach these concepts to all our budding superflexible thinkers. It's important for everyone who uses these books to make sure that kids understand that *every* superhero (including his or her own Superflex) must learn to use these critical powers to maximize their flexible thinking.

The Saga of How Superflex Got His Powers (and how you can acquire your powers too!)

Defeating Unthinkables has always been one of the greatest challenges of all humankind. This is because Unthinkables are sneaky and powerful and, just when we think we've laid them all to rest, another one pops onto the scene. All of us (kids and adults alike) must always be ready to defeat these foes, which means we need to learn some extra powers of our own.

Luckily, there's a special formula we can all use when faced with any Unthinkable. This formula has been passed from Superflex to Superflex over the ages — and Aiden's Superflex is about to disclose this secret.

INTRODUCTION
CHAPTER 1 © 2012 SOCIAL THINKING PUBLISHING

We invite you, as Superflex Academy students, to prepare yourselves to learn about Superflex's Very Cool Five-Step Power Plan!

When you read the original Superflex comic book, *Superflex Takes on Rock Brain and the Team of Unthinkables*, you probably noticed that Aiden's Superflex had some pretty amazing abilities to defeat his Unthinkables. That's because his Superflex had already learned and developed these powers and was using the Very Cool Five-Step Power Plan. So, it's time to get your students' brains ready to learn the secrets necessary to train their own superflexible thinking!

Superflex's (and Our) Very Cool Five-Step Power Plan

First, here's how this plan came about: Superflex learned about the five critical powers needed to defeat Unthinkables from five of his pals, who each shared one special lesson or power. These Power Pals — Decider, Social Detective, Brakester, Flex DoBody, and Cranium Coach — came together with Superflex's guidance to think as a team to create true superflexible thinking. These lessons are called the **Very Cool Five-Step Power Plan**. It's now available throughout Social Town for teachers, parents, and students to help defeat their own Unthinkables.

We all know that defeating Unthinkables takes an organized plan with steps to follow. That's how Aiden's Superflex took on Rock Brain, Brain Eater, and the others. Here are the lessons Superflex learned from each of the Power Pals:

DECIDER © provides **Power #1,** the ability to **stop, decide,** and **describe** which Unthinkable(s) is trying to overpower your superflexible thinking.

Decider taught Superflex how to **stop** and **describe** what was happening within the student's body and brain so that Superflex and the student could decide which Unthinkable was attempting to invade. Once the Unthinkable was identified, Decider helped Superflex better use his other powers. As Decider explained to Superflex, it doesn't make sense to use a strategy designed to defeat Mean Jean if he was trying to defeat WasFunnyOnce!

SOCIAL DETECTIVE © provides **Power #2,** the ability to **stop** and **observe** the situation and the people in the situation.

Social Detective took the time to show Superflex that a critical power lies within everyone's own observation toolbox. Social Detective taught Superflex about using **clues** from his eyes, ears, and brain to help understand the situation and the people in the situation. Wow! This was amazingly helpful to Superflex because it helped him develop super-sensitive observation powers (a whole surveillance system) in his brain.

BRAKESTER© provides **Power #3,** the power to **stop** and **think** to discover the hidden rules.

Brakester has always worked closely with Social Detective, and the two even have an office in the same Social Town building. Over the years, Brakester and Social Detective often talked of how their special powers should ultimately combine for the greater good of all Social Town citizens. So before sharing Power #3 with Superflex, Brakester made sure that Superflex had first paid a visit to Social Detective to learn about observation. Brakester then taught Superflex how he could **stop** and **think** about the hidden rules once he'd observed the people in the situation. Brakester talked about how the hidden rules are almost like hidden treasures because they're the secrets of the social situation and help to explain why people are expected to act in certain ways! Superflex was very excited to gain this power.

FLEX DoBODY© provides **Power #4,** flex and do, the power to **use flexible thinking** to determine strategies to use **to do** what's expected.

Flex DoBody spent many years at the Social Town Community Center teaching the adults of Social Town how to be flexible, make good choices, and do the right thing! It was there that he passed by Superflex, Decider, Social Detective, and Brakester while they were having a meeting to discuss their powers. It was then that Flex DoBody knew the time was right to show them the importance of another special power. Flex showed Superflex things he must practice each day to learn to flexibly pick the best choice to make at the right time and in the right place. Then Flex gave Superflex a test by saying: "Now that you've described your Unthinkable, observed the situation, and stopped to think about what's expected, what strategies will you **flex**ibly think about? Which one or two will you choose to **do** to defeat this scoundrel?" Superflex realized that Flex was teaching him the secret of **flex** and **do**! Superflex understood that thinking and observing are super important but using flexible thinking, making choices, and carrying out a plan to defeat an Unthinkable are also important. This power helps Superflex finish any job he's started!

CRANIUM COACH© provides **Power #5,** using **self-talk** with help from your built-in brain coach! (Remember: This coach is usually in your brain and just silently coaches you.)

Superflex made a final visit to his very wise pal, Cranium Coach. The coach had heard from the other Power Pals that Superflex was on his way to learn how to use the final **power** in the Very Cool Five-Step Power Plan. Cranium Coach explained to Superflex that everyone needs to hear when they "did a good job" or when they need to "hang in there" or "keep trying." Cranium Coach revealed to Superflex that everyone actually has a built-in inner brain coach. From Cranium Coach, Superflex learned how to use his inner brain coach to motivate himself to keep working to defeat whatever Unthinkable was near **or** to call on a Thinkable when necessary. (See the next section to learn about Thinkables.) This was exactly what Superflex needed to know — that he had his very own built-in inner coach who would **silently** coach him throughout the day. (Oh, and by the way, Superflex didn't know what "cranium" meant so he asked another friend, who explained "cranium" is another word used to refer to a person's brain.)

People use Cranium Coach's special power to encourage themselves to notice when they're doing something well or when they need to coach themselves to keep trying because they're not quite done with the task yet!

You can go ahead and tell yourself "good job" when you use any of the powers just described even if you weren't able to fully defeat your Unthinkable. Cranium Coach helps you notice that you're improving even if you aren't great at it yet! And, you can also use your coach to help you describe the things you did that helped you through the process!

Let's Review

Here are the five powers that together make up the Very Cool Five-Step Power Plan.

Superflex's Power Pals	Powers for the Very Cool Five-Step Power Plan
Decider	1. Stop, decide, and describe your Unthinkable
Social Detective	2. Observe the situation and people in it
Brakester	3. Stop and think about the hidden rules
Flex DoBody	4. Flex and do your strategy
Cranium Coach	5. Use self-talk to tell yourself you've done well

That's it!

Now you can teach your students the secrets to helping them develop their own Superflex to be as powerful as possible. But, just like Aiden's Superflex, all students must be willing to go to the Superflex Academy to build up their powers. In the next chapter (and on the CD that comes with the book) you'll find a handout you can use with your students to introduce them to the Very Cool Five-Step Power Plan.

What's a Thinkable?

We noticed that our citizens of Social Town were accomplishing some great feats by learning how to monitor the Unthinkables who were trying to control their brains and by using strategies to keep their superflexible thinking in control. Some citizens became so good at making choices to keep Superflex in charge of their brain that one or more of their Unthinkables were mostly defeated most of the time! This meant that their Unthinkable thinking wasn't showing up to really challenge Superflex anymore. The Town Council of Social Town found this very exciting! With Superflex keeping control of their minds, those citizens were now more easily slipping into good-choice thinking without having to start by defeating Unthinkables. As they observed this happening more and more, the Town Council began to celebrate the developing Thinkables, which meant they didn't have to spend so much of the city's budget and time on the Unthinkables!

Chapter 5 introduces some Thinkables that have begun to be created as citizens shift their focus away from their Unthinkables. You'll notice that there aren't as many Thinkables as there are Unthinkables. This is because only recently have our citizens been able to learn to acquire that much Superflex brain power! Teachers, counselors, and parents in Social Town are encouraged to help their students develop their own Thinkables each time they've been able to put an Unthinkable to rest for an ongoing period of time. Everyone likes a celebration, and the creation of Thinkables is one more way to celebrate our citizens' progress.

Being Flexible—Another Use of Thinkables
(for students who focus too much attention on the negative powers of the Unthinkables)

After the Thinkables began to show up in the strong new powerful thinking of our Social Town citizens, the Town Council was presented with a proposal to consider an alternative use of the Thinkables. It had come to the attention of the Council that some Social Town citizens were having so much fun talking about the Unthinkables and demonstrating their negative powers that they weren't learning from Superflex. Instead, the Unthinkables had become even more powerful in their brains! With this select group of students, adults are now encouraged to **avoid using Unthinkables** altogether and to **only** focus on teaching this type of student to develop a Thinkable pathway to superflexible thinking. While the Town Council knows it's more fun for our citizens to defeat the Unthinkables rather than simply create the thinking powers associated with the Thinkables, some students can't cope with the compare and contrast style of learning presented by Superflex and the Team of Unthinkables. For these select students, we strongly encourage you to teach them in a special club where they learn about Superflex and building his Team of Thinkables.

The Social Town caregivers can use the template included in the next chapter and on the CD to help our young citizens develop more and more Thinkables. A Thinkable can celebrate the defeat of an Unthinkable or be used as an alternative to talking about Unthinkables as described.

CHAPTER 2
Using This Information with Your Students

This chapter discusses how you can use the materials in the book with your students and includes handouts/templates for them as well.

Using This Information with Your Students

Our goal in bringing this new book in the Superflex series to life is to continue to find cool ways to encourage our students to think about their own thinking, how their behaviors are interpreted by others and to provide them with more strategies to use. After introducing our brand new strategy, the **Very Cool Five-Step Power Plan,** we provide numerous examples of how it's used "in action" through the introduction of 82 new Unthinkables and 14 Thinkables characters. Once students learn the steps to the Power Plan, they can explore any of the characters in any order to help them learn more about themselves and the social thinking and behavioral regulation challenges they face. It is not expected that students or educators, counselors and parents become familiar with all 96 new characters.

The five handouts included in this chapter (and on the CD for easy duplication) reinforce the concepts and make learning a hands-on experience for students. They will help you encourage your students to come up with their own Unthinkables and Thinkables that match their particular needs. Educators, counselors, and parents can also use the material to expand how they teach students to self-coach, self-monitor, and self-regulate their own behavior when around others.

In expanding our approach to teach students how Superflex became so superflexible, we realize we are teaching a more complicated thinking process to children. Based on feedback from our Social Town Adults, we are now conservatively recommending that this revised Superflex material is best used with third to fifth graders. We realize people are using Superflex with younger students and that the concepts are very well received with neurotypical learners. However, our young students with social thinking challenges often find the demands that the Superflex concepts impose upon their weak self-regulation system to be overwhelming, leading to a system shut-down. For this reason we are encouraging educators, counselors and parents to be very cautious about who they use these new materials with if the student is younger than a 3rd grade classroom placement or is in a self-contained classroom. In fact, they should be careful how this material is used by any student. We never want any of our lessons to set a child up for further social regulation failure!

We hope our work and the contributions we gathered from our Social Town Citizens inspires other original and respectful ways to tackle the social regulation problems experienced by our students (and… our spouses, partners, and co-workers too ☺).

How the Information Is Organized

Both this chapter and the CD that comes with this book include the handout for introducing your students to the Very Cool Five-Step Power Plan. The chapter and the CD also include the Power Plan Defeat Handout that students can use to discover their own Unthinkables, and the Create Your Own Thinkable Handout for them to create Thinkables, and a handout for drawing their creations. The Thoughts of Social Town Citizens handout at the end of this chapter and on the CD can be used as a worksheet for students to develop perspective taking about how other citizens might view expected and unexpected behaviors to relate to a certain Unthinkable or Thinkable. You can reproduce the handouts from the book or use the files for these items on the CD.

Chapter 3 shows how Superflex is using the **Very Cool Five-Step Power Plan** to help defeat each of the 14 original Unthinkables.

Chapters 4 and 5 present the new Unthinkables and Thinkables that have been contributed by Social Town authors of all ages. Some of these Unthinkables and Thinkables addressed a similar general issue or dilemma. We purposefully selected these because they represent diverse ways citizens may look at and tackle that general topic. That's why you'll find that we have grouped the Unthinkables and Thinkables by theme or category. Some of these categories have more than one Unthinkable or Thinkable, such as "Following Rules Too Closely," and others have just one, such as "I'm Bored."

For each category, we've **arbitrarily** selected one Unthinkable or Thinkable to expand upon to show how to apply the new teaching approach of Superflex's Very Cool Five-Step Power Plan. The reader will find the shorter version of this power plan printed in the book. This is material for the student to review with an adult.

We also wrote an expanded teacher/parent version for the arbitrarily selected Unthinkables and Thinkables, which you'll find on the CD. The purpose of this expanded version is to provide teachers, counselors, and parents with more information they may choose to explore with their students. In some of these expanded sections, we note extra resources caregivers can go access to learn more strategies related to these concepts. These pages include a thought bubble with Thoughts of Social Town citizens to present the citizens' perspective on the topic.

CHAPTER 2 © 2012 SOCIAL THINKING PUBLISHING

Any additional Unthinkables or Thinkables in that category are presented as the authors provided them, with only minor edits. Expanding some and not others doesn't mean we thought any one was better than any other! We don't want Grump Grumpaniny to emerge here — especially for our junior authors!

Chapter 6 acknowledges all contributors and shares more information about them, based on parent permission for our younger authors.

Chapter 7 is a Glossary that defines some of the more recent key Social Thinking Vocabulary terms used throughout the book. Note that this isn't an extensive vocabulary list; it's expected that readers of this book have already had extensive learning and experience with Social Thinking terminology.

The Bibliography in Chapter 8 offers suggested resources to learn more about the concepts and strategies presented here.

About the CD

You can use the resources included on the CD to support teaching and learning about Superflex. The purpose of the CD is two-fold. First, we wanted to give you an easy way to reproduce the materials from the book, and second, it contains extra content for the adult reader.

The illustrations for each new Unthinkable and Thinkable submitted by Social Town Citizens are included as separate files that you can project or copy for your students. We also included an illustration of Superflex, since so many of you are finding creative ways to teach superflexible thinking in your classrooms.

The student handouts included in this chapter are included on the CD as well. You can print these and hand them out to students.

The expanded sections for selected Unthinkables and Thinkables that are described earlier in this chapter are also provided on the CD. You can use these for more in-depth teaching about specific Unthinkables or Thinkables, using the Very Cool Five-Step Power Plan. These are appropriate to share as handouts only with students who have more advanced skills; otherwise, we recommend you use them as a tool for your own teaching.

Superflex's Very Cool Five-Step Power Plan

Here's how Superflex learned the powers of his Power Pals and came up with the Very Cool Five-Step Power Plan:

Can you use the Very Cool Five-Step Power Plan to defeat your own Unthinkables? Yes! You can use a "Power Plan Defeat Handout" to develop a plan to defeat your Unthinkables! And you can use a "Create Your Own Thinkable Handout" to identify new Thinkables.

Decider provides Power #1. **Decider** taught Superflex that if he isn't sure which Unthinkable or Unthinkables are in his brain, he needs to "call in the reinforcements." This means to **get some help from someone!**

Use **Decider** to **stop**, **decide**, and **describe** which Unthinkable is trying to overpower your Superflex! Sometimes (in fact, most of the time), there's more than one Unthinkable.

Your job is to ask a teacher, a parent, or someone else to help you decide which Unthinkable you're trying to defeat if you're not sure. This step in the power plan is one of the most critical because it guides what strategies (or what Thinkables) you may need to call on for maximum flexible thinking.

Social Detective provides Power #2: Use your **Social Detective** whenever you go into a social situation and call on your observation skills by using your detective toolbox. This will help you gather all of the critical clues to move to the next step.

Brakester provides Power #3: Use **Brakester** once you've used your detective tools. You'll then be able to **stop** and **think** about the hidden rules. This will help you figure out what the expected behaviors are for the situation.

Flex DoBody provides Power #4: Use this **flex** and **do** power after you've described, decided, observed, and thought about the expected behaviors for the situation. Then, you're ready to **use flexible thinking** to choose the right strategy or strategies **to do** what's expected.

Cranium Coach provides Power #5: Use **Cranium Coach** to encourage yourself to notice when you're doing something well or when you need to coach yourself to keep trying because you're not quite done with the task yet! Go ahead and tell yourself "good job" when you use any of the first four powers just described even if you weren't able to fully defeat your Unthinkable. You can use Cranium Coach to help you notice that you're improving even if you're not great at it yet! And, you can also use your coach to help you describe the things you did that helped you through the process!

Let's Review

Here are the five powers that together make up the Very Cool Five-Step Power Plan.

Superflex's Power Pals	Powers for the Very Cool Five-Step Power Plan
Decider	1. Stop, decide, and describe your Unthinkable
Social Detective	2. Observe the situation and people in it
Brakester	3. Stop and think about the hidden rules
Flex DoBody	4. Flex and do your strategy
Cranium Coach	5. Use self-talk to tell yourself you've done well

Stop! **Which Unthinkable** is invading your brain?
Use Superflex's **Very Cool Five-Step Power Plan** to identify and conquer.

Power #1: The Decider power helps you to **stop, describe,** and **decide** the powers of the Unthinkable.

·

Power #2: The Social Detective power helps you to **observe** the situation and the people in the situation.

·

Power #3: The Brakester power helps you to **stop** and **think** to discover the hidden rules.

·

Power #4: The Flex Do-Body power helps you to **use flexible thinking** to choose strategies to use **to do** what's expected.

a.

b.

c.

Power #5: The Cranium Coach power helps remind you to **use your self-talk** to tell yourself you've done well using new strategies.

YOU CAN DO IT!

You can tell you've done this today when you can say to yourself:

USING THIS INFORMATION WITH YOUR STUDENTS
CHAPTER 2 © 2012 SOCIAL THINKING PUBLISHING

Wow! **Which Thinkable** wants to give your brain superflexible, super organized power?
Use Superflex's **Very Cool Five-Step Power Plan** to help you focus on your Thinkable and keep Unthinkables away.

Power #1: **The Decider** power helps you to stop, describe, and **decide** the powers of the Unthinkable.

•

Now that you know that you're calling on the Thinkable _____, discover how the next four powers boost your Thinkable's powers.

Power #2: **The Social Detective** power helps you to **observe** the situation and the people in the situation.

•

Power #3: **The Brakester** power helps you to **stop** and **think** to discover the hidden rules.

•

Power #4: **The Flex Do-Body** power helps you to **use flexible thinking** to choose strategies to use **to do** what's expected.

a.

b.

c.

Power #5: **The Cranium Coach** power helps remind you to **use your self-talk** to tell yourself you've done well using new strategies.

You can tell you've done this today when you can say to yourself:

Draw Your Unthinkable or Thinkable Here

USING THIS INFORMATION WITH YOUR STUDENTS

Thoughts of Social Town Citizens

CHAPTER 3

The Original Team of Unthinkables and the Very Cool Five-Step Power Plan

The following pages show how Superflex is using his
newly acquired powers to help defeat each of the
14 original Unthinkables.

Stop! *Body Snatcher* is invading your brain!
Use Superflex's Very Cool Five-Step Power Plan to defeat this Unthinkable.

Power #1: The Decider power helps you to **stop, describe,** and **decide** the powers of the Unthinkable.

Body Snatcher

- **Body Snatcher** gets a person to move his or her body away from the group the person is expected to participate in, such as in class or a group conversation.

Power #2: The Social Detective power helps you to **observe** the situation and the people in the situation.

- Your Social Detective observes how people use their bodies as one way to show they're sharing space in the group, are paying attention, and are interested in what's happening in a group.

Power #3: The Brakester power helps you to **stop** and **think** to discover the hidden rules.

- People always try to think about what their head, shoulders, hips, and feet need to be doing so they show interest with their body position. When they're a part of a group, it's expected that citizens face the others in the group by keeping their head, shoulders, hips, and feet in the direction of the other group members.

Power #4: The Flex Do-Body power helps you to **use flexible thinking** to choose strategies to use **to do** what's expected.

a. In class, if you're unsure if you can get up to do something, think with your eyes and find the clues that show you it's okay to get up and move away from the group. For example, one clue is that the teacher is sitting at her desk and isn't talking to the whole class. If you've searched for clues but are still unsure if it's okay to get up, raise your hand and ask the teacher.

b. Imagine that you have special social glue on the soles of your shoes that helps keep you in the group. It also helps you think about if the people in the group see you as trying to stick with the group or get away from it.

c. Keep in mind the "shoulder rules":
- When walking with others, one shoulder should line up with the other person's shoulder.
- When standing with others, your shoulders should face the whole group.

Power #5: The Cranium Coach power helps remind you to **use your self-talk** to tell yourself you've done well using new strategies.

- You can tell you've done this today when you can say to yourself:
"People around me appear comfortable that I'm thinking about them with my body. I've noticed that I'm able to stay connected longer with others. My teacher may even compliment me on the great job I'm doing of keeping my body with the group."

Stop! *Brain Eater* is invading your brain!
Use Superflex's Very Cool Five-Step Power Plan to defeat this Unthinkable.

Power #1: The Decider power helps you to **stop, describe, and decide** the powers of the Unthinkable.

- **Brain Eater** invades people's thinking and distracts them with their own personal thoughts or with things around the room that suddenly seem more interesting than what they're supposed to be paying attention to. Brain Eater loves to appear in the morning to make it harder for students to get ready for school on time.

Brain Eater

Power #2: The Social Detective power helps you to **observe** the situation and the people in the situation.

- Your Social Detective notices that most people can defeat Brain Eater quite easily when they're in the classroom or having a conversation. Sometimes in class, students' brains wander away from the topic, but they catch themselves and remember to focus again on what the teacher is talking about so they don't miss anything important.

Power #3: The Brakester power helps you to **stop** and **think** to discover the hidden rules.

- It's expected that students try to keep their brain focused when the teacher is teaching and at any other time when someone is talking with them and thinking about them. Citizens are often aware of what can distract their brains and try to avoid focusing on those things.

Power #4: The Flex Do-Body power helps you to **use flexible thinking** to choose strategies to use **to do** what's expected.

a. Learn more about Superflex strategies to defeat Brain Eater by reading the book *Superflex Takes on Brain Eater* with your family or teacher.
b. A therapist at school called an occupational therapist can help you learn ways to keep your brain more focused.
c. Use strategies like checklists and schedules to help you see what you may need to focus on to get yourself ready for school in the morning. Work with an adult to find ways to break a job into small parts and then reward yourself for finishing each part.
d. Use a timer to help you know how long you can and will stay focused on a task before taking a break.

Power #5: The Cranium Coach power helps remind you to **use your self-talk** to tell yourself you've done well using new strategies.

- You can tell you've done this today when you can say to yourself: "I notice when my brain is on track and listening to teachers or citizens when they're talking. I'm catching myself when my brain starts to think about something different."

Stop! **D.O.F. The Destroyer of Fun**

is invading your brain!

Use Superflex's Very Cool Five-Step Power Plan to defeat this Unthinkable.

Power #1: **The Decider** power helps you to **stop, describe,** and **decide** the powers of the Unthinkable.

- **D.O.F. The Destroyer of Fun** makes people overly competitive. This Unthinkable likes to hang around activities when people compete — like board games and sports — and get them really upset if they're not doing as well playing the game as they think they should.

D.O.F. - The Destroyer of Fun

Power #2: **The Social Detective** power helps you to **observe** the situation and the people in the situation.

- Your Social Detective observes that during activities like board games, everyone mostly enjoys their time together and manages to feel okay even if they lose. During sports activities, your Social Detective sees that many citizens want to win and they show their excitement when that happens. But citizens also know there's only one "winner" and that's simply part of playing the game. They know that it's important to consider the thoughts and feelings of the other players too. This is called "good sportsmanship."

Power #3: **The Brakester** power helps you to **stop** and **think** to discover the hidden rules.

- It's expected that people who play games or sports with others support their teammates by cheering for them, complimenting them, and watching them as they take a turn or make a play. Citizens like to play with people who look calm and act like they enjoy being with others even if they're not winning.

Power #4: **The Flex Do-Body** power helps you to **use flexible thinking** to choose strategies to use **to do** what's expected.

a. When you play a game, think about ways you can be flexible and show that you're a good sport. Examples are letting someone else go first or compromising on what game to play.

b. If a game isn't going the way you want it to go, stay calm and use self-talk to remind yourself it's nice to be playing with others.

c. Remember to add friendly thoughts during the game to show the other people in the group that you're thinking about them. Some examples might be, "Nice shot, you'll get it next time," and "That was close, great game!"

Power #5: **The Cranium Coach** power helps remind you to **use your self-talk** to tell yourself you've done well using new strategies.

- You can tell you've done this today when you can say to yourself:
"Teachers and adults give me positive compliments about my sportsmanship and flexibility. Other students ask me to play with them or select me for their teams."

Stop! Energy Hare-y is invading your brain!
Use Superflex's Very Cool Five-Step Power Plan to defeat this Unthinkable.

Energy Hare-y

Power #1: The Decider power helps you to **stop, describe,** and **decide** the powers of the Unthinkable.

- **Energy Hare-y** gives people too much energy, especially at times when their bodies should be calm. People then find it hard to calm down. The longer Energy Hare-y is in charge of someone's thinking and body, the more active the person gets.

Power #2: The Social Detective power helps you to **observe** the situation and the people in the situation.

- Your Social Detective sees that in a classroom, the energy level is usually pretty low, and at recess, it's usually pretty high.

Power #3: The Brakester power helps you to **stop** and **think** to discover the hidden rules.

- Citizens always think about the energy level expected in the situation and observe the energy level used by the people around them. When a person's energy level matches what's expected in the situation, this helps citizens feel comfortable being near this person.

Power #4: The Flex Do-Body power helps you to **use flexible thinking** to choose strategies to use **to do** what's expected.

a. Use your Social Detective to see if your energy level matches what's expected for the situation and of the others around you. If you find it really hard to do this, an occupational therapist at your school can help you learn how and give you tools to help you stay calm. One way might be using a fidget, a small item that you can have in your hands under the table.
b. Use a timer to set how long you'll try to keep your body calm while working in the classroom. Your teacher can help with this.
c. When your body has too much energy, check with your teacher about going to a place in the classroom where you can take some breaths and calm your body.
d. If you know you'll be going into a situation where you need to be calm, first try to do something active to get out your energy like going up and down stairs, walking, or running.

Power #5: The Cranium Coach power helps remind you to **use your self-talk** to tell yourself you've done well using new strategies.

- You can tell you've done this today when you can say to yourself:
"I'm doing a good job staying in control of my body and energy level. It may not be easy for me all the time but I notice that I'm trying to use tools to help me."

Stop! **Glassman** is invading your brain!
Use Superflex's Very Cool Five-Step Power Plan to defeat this Unthinkable.

Power #1: The Decider power helps you to **stop, describe,** and **decide** the powers of the Unthinkable.

- **Glassman** makes people have huge upset reactions to problems. Glassman loves to tag team with Rock Brain to cause problems all over Social Town. Rock Brain starts by getting citizens stuck on thinking that something has to be done their way, even when it's a small problem. If that doesn't happen, Glassman steps in and gets citizens to have a huge upset about this tiny problem.

Glassman

Power #2: The Social Detective power helps you to **observe** the situation and the people in the situation.

- Your Social Detective sees that citizens respond to things in different ways and with different emotions. Even though people have all sorts of feelings, as they get to be school age, they learn to respond to situations with small to no reaction. Doing this keeps themselves and others feeling comfortable.

Power #3: The Brakester power helps you to **stop** and **think** to discover the hidden rules.

- Citizens are expected to share their emotions in small ways, like using their words to tell someone calmly how they're feeling, why they're frustrated, or to describe a problem. It's expected that people may get frustrated or mad from time to time but that they'll usually make their emotional reaction smaller and stay in control.

Power #4: The Flex Do-Body power helps you to **use flexible thinking** to choose strategies to use **to do** what's expected.

a. Your teachers can help you learn more about strategies to control your emotions.
b. Explore the size of the problem that's bothering you. If you realize that the problem is small, you can have a more expected reaction like letting it go, ignoring it, or choosing to calmly talk to someone about it.
c. If you're with others and start to get frustrated, let them know that you need to take a short break. Take yourself somewhere quiet and try to take some deep breaths and think about your other strategies to prevent this Glassman moment.

Power #5: The Cranium Coach power helps remind you to **use your self-talk** to tell yourself you've done well using new strategies.

- You can tell you've done this today when you can say to yourself:
"I'm finding myself staying calm and more in control of my emotions. Also, I see that people are seeking me out to play or hang out and adults are complimenting me on my staying in control."

Stop! Grump Grumpaniny is invading your brain!
Use Superflex's Very Cool Five-Step Power Plan to defeat this Unthinkable.

Power #1: **The Decider** power helps you to **stop, describe,** and **decide** the powers of the Unthinkable.

- **Grump Grumpaniny** puts people in grumpy moods and over the smallest things.

Power #2: **The Social Detective** power helps you to **observe** the situation and the people in the situation.

Grump Grumpaniny

- Your Social Detective notices that others try to seem happy or appear friendly most of the time even when they might be having a tough day. This is because they know that if they seem unhappy, it makes others feel uncomfortable. Your detective may also observe that emotions are kind of contagious — when one person is grumpy, it starts to make others not feel so good.

Power #3: **The Brakester** power helps you to **stop** and **think** to discover the hidden rules.

- Citizens are expected to work at trying to stay positive and appear friendly when they're around others, including their family members. However, in most families people can be flexible in expressing how they feel because they live together. Family members still try to work at staying positive when that's possible because being grumpy can affect all the other people in the house.
- When citizens have an activity or a task that they don't want to do or that they think might not be fun, it's expected that they use their thinking to keep them positive and motivated to get through the task. If they get stuck in a grumpy cycle, it makes the task harder.

Power #4: **The Flex Do-Body** power helps you to **use flexible thinking** to choose strategies to use **to do** what's expected.

a. If you have to do something that you don't like or don't want to do and see yourself heading down the grumpy path, think about how you look to others. Break down a task into smaller parts so that you don't see it as such a big job.
b. If you seem to be grumpy or down a lot, you may want to talk to your parent, teacher, or therapist about it so they can help you.
c. Make a journal of things that make you feel good. Then when you catch yourself getting down and grumpy about something, look at your book to help you stay positive and move through it.

Power #5: **The Cranium Coach** power helps remind you to **use your self-talk** to tell yourself you've done well using new strategies.

- You can tell you've done this today when you can say to yourself:
  "I'm trying to see things more positively and not let things get me down so easily. I may notice others including me in activities because they're more comfortable with me."

Stop! Mean Jean is invading your brain!
Use Superflex's Very Cool Five-Step Power Plan to defeat this Unthinkable.

Power #1: **The Decider** power helps you to **stop, describe,** and **decide** the powers of the Unthinkable.

- **Mean Jean** gets people to act mean and bossy toward others.

Power #2: The Social Detective power helps you to **observe** the situation and the people in the situation.

- Your Social Detective sees that most people get along quite well. This is because they're always thinking about how others might feel so they avoid saying things that might be thought of as mean, hurtful, or bossy. At times, people might have a mean or a bossy thought, but they keep that thought in their brain.

Mean Jean

Power #3: The Brakester power helps you to **stop** and **think** to discover the hidden rules.

- When citizens want someone to do something, it's expected they say so in a way that keeps the person feeling comfortable. One way to do this is to try to ask for something instead of just telling the person what you want.

Power #4: The Flex Do-Body power helps you to **use flexible thinking** to choose strategies to use **to do** what's expected.

a. If you have a mean thought about someone, turn on your brain filter, which only lets thoughts through the filter that help others to feel okay or even good. This imaginary device keeps your mean or bossy words trapped in your mind and lets the friendly words out.

b. If you know which situations are the most likely for Mean Jean to pop in for a visit, remind yourself to work extra hard at those times to use your filter and to think about how others will be thinking about what you say to them!

c. To help you stay calm, take a calming breath and use self-talk. You can do this by stopping, taking a long deep breath, and thinking: "These words won't make that person feel good so I need to keep them in my brain. The other person may think I'm mean if I let this thought out of my brain." Then try to move on.

d. If you sometimes want to say mean things to people when you're feeling angry at them, you could work with your teachers to learn more about understanding your feelings so you can try and stay in control with how you act around others.

Power #5: The Cranium Coach power helps remind you to **use your self-talk** to tell yourself you've done well using new strategies.

- You can tell you've done this today when you can say to yourself:
  "I notice that I'm not being so mean or bossy with my words and I'm better at filtering my thoughts."

Stop! One-Sided Sid is invading your brain!

Use Superflex's Very Cool Five-Step Power Plan to defeat this Unthinkable.

Power #1: **The Decider** power helps you to **stop, describe,** and **decide** the powers of the Unthinkable.

- **One-Sided Sid** gets people to talk only about themselves.

Power #2: **The Social Detective** power helps you to **observe** the situation and the people in the situation.

- Your Social Detective observes that citizens enjoy learning about others when they hang out by asking questions about the others and listening to people's comments.

Power #3: **The Brakester** power helps you to **stop** and **think** to discover the hidden rules.

One-Sided Sid

- It's expected that when citizens talk to each other socially, they show interest in the people in the group and think about how to include others in the conversation. Citizens love to share information about themselves but know they should only share a little bit of information at a time. There needs to be a balance of talking time among people in a conversation so everyone can feel important.
- Because conversations jump around to different topics, it's possible that people may not be totally interested in a topic. When this happens, it's expected that citizens pretend and look like it's a topic they want to hear about. This is called doing the "social fake" and is something good social thinkers learn to do pretty well. It's unexpected for people to keep bringing the conversation back to what they want to talk about all the time or even to say out loud that a topic is boring to them.

Power #4: **The Flex Do-Body** power helps you to **use flexible thinking** to choose strategies to use **to do** what's expected.

a. Use your people file tool, an imaginary file in your brain that you can use to keep information that you learn about a friend, classmate, or anyone else. In future conversations, you can open that file and remember a topic or hobby the person is interested in and then ask a question about it.

b. If you're not sure what to ask someone, use the imaginary flip it tool to ask the person something similar to what the citizen asked you. For example, if someone says, "Have you seen any good movies lately?," you can flip it and ask, "Have you?"

c. Learn more about the social fake. Using it makes others feel like you're comfortable with what they're talking about and that keeps them thinking you're friendly or interested in them.

Power #5: **The Cranium Coach** power helps remind you to **use your self-talk** to tell yourself you've done well using new strategies.

- You can tell you've done this today when you can say to yourself:
"I'm able to learn new information about people I'm with and they seem to truly enjoy being with me."

stop! Rock Brain is invading your brain!
Use Superflex's Very Cool Five-Step Power Plan to defeat this Unthinkable.

Power #1: **The Decider** power helps you to **stop, describe,** and **decide** the powers of the Unthinkable.

- **Rock Brain** gets people stuck on their ideas. This makes it hard for them to be good problem solvers and to think about others.

Power #2: **The Social Detective** power helps you to **observe** the situation and the people in the situation.

Rock Brain

- Your Social Detective notices those situations that call for flexible thinking. This might happen when you're with others and people need to offer their ideas and agree on what to do together, like when you work on a group project.
- Your Social Detective also is aware that your daily activities may change for many reasons. Your detective sees how easily people adjust their plans for others and for themselves. Someone might get a little frustrated with a change but then quickly goes with the flow of what's happening.

Power #3: **The Brakester** power helps you to **stop** and **think** to discover the hidden rules.

- It's expected that every citizen will have to deal with moments of change and being flexible. This is part of living with other citizens in your Social Town. Imagine what it would be like if no one could be flexible and go with someone else's plan or idea. Social Town wouldn't be much fun at all!

Power #4: **The Flex Do-Body** power helps you to **use flexible thinking** to choose strategies to use **to do** what's expected.

a. When there are changes in your routine, think about the size of the problem. Your teachers can help you learn how to map out your problems on a problem solving scale. The more you can learn about the size of your different problems and how to be the most flexible with smaller size problems, the more you can help yourself defeat Rock Brain!

b. Use positive self-talk to get through a flexible thinking moment. For example: "I really want to play my video game, but I know that my mom needs to get to her doctor's appointment. Turning off my game is really a tiny problem because I can save it and come back to it another time. If I can be flexible, this will give my mom good thoughts and she won't have to worry about being on time."

Power #5: **The Cranium Coach** power helps remind you to **use your self-talk** to tell yourself you've done well using new strategies.

- You can tell you've done this today when you can say to yourself:
"I'm able to think about different ways to approach a situation or consider different ideas and then create a plan that helps me and others around me stay calm."

Stop! Space Invader is invading your brain!
Use Superflex's Very Cool Five-Step Power Plan to defeat this Unthinkable.

Power #1: The **Decider** power helps you to **stop, describe,** and **decide** the powers of the Unthinkable.

- **Space Invader** gets people to stand too close to others and move into other people's space because they're unaware of how close is too close.

Power #2: The **Social Detective** power helps you to **observe** the situation and the people in the situation.

Space Invader

- Your Social Detective notices that when people are together, they're often about one arm's length away from each other and have their head, hips, shoulders, and feet facing the people they're talking to. Also, citizens seem to have this invisible bubble around them, which is called "personal space." When someone is unaware of how close they are to someone else, this can cause the other person to feel really uncomfortable.
- Your detective notices that sometimes this space gets smaller and it's okay to be closer to people like when standing in the lunch line or sitting with a group at a table. The bubble may also become smaller when people are with others they know well, like parents, siblings, or close friends.

Power #3: The **Brakester** power helps you to **stop** and **think** to discover the hidden rules.

- It's expected that people stop to think about how close or far away they should stand from someone based on the situation and how well they know the person.

Power #4: The **Flex Do-Body** power helps you to **use flexible thinking** to choose strategies to use **to do** what's expected.

a. Observe how people stand in groups and how their bodies are pretty organized about how far from or close they are to another person. Practice using the one-arm rule and standing with your head, hips, shoulders, and feet pointed toward the people you're with.
b. Use self-talk at school or when with friends to help you think about how close you should be: "We're all talking in a group, so I should be about an arm's length away."
c. Notice if people often take steps to move a little bit away from you when you interact with them. If they do, this may mean you're invading their space. If you notice people keep taking steps to get closer to you, this means they think you're standing too far away from them.

Power #5: The **Cranium Coach** power helps remind you to **use your self-talk** to tell yourself you've done well using new strategies.

- You can tell you've done this today when you can say to yourself:
"I'm using my strategy of the one-arm rule and how to position my body when I'm around others, and I notice that people are feeling more calm and comfortable around me."

Stop! Topic Twistermeister is invading your brain!
Use Superflex's Very Cool Five-Step Power Plan to defeat this Unthinkable.

Topic Twistermeister

Power #1: The **Decider** power helps you to **stop, describe,** and **decide** the powers of the Unthinkable.

- **Topic Twistermeister** gets citizens so stuck on their random thoughts that they make comments that seem to others like whopping topic changes.

Power #2: The **Social Detective** power helps you to **observe** the situation and the people in the situation.

- Your Social Detective notices that when citizens talk to one another, they follow the main idea of the conversation and add thoughts or ask questions that are related to the shifting topics. This helps the conversation flow in a clear way so everyone can follow along. When someone says something that's off the topic, that means other people can't figure out how it's related to what people were talking about before and this can make people confused.

Power #3: The **Brakester** power helps you to **stop** and **think** to discover the hidden rules.

- When citizens are around others, it's expected that people stay connected and follow the flow of what citizens are saying to each other. When people want to add something, they make a comment or ask a question that closely relates to what was just said and the larger topic of the conversation.

Power #4: The **Flex Do-Body** power helps you to **use flexible thinking** to choose strategies to use **to do** what's expected.

a. Ask yourself: "Will my comment relate back to the topic we're talking about?" If the answer is no, keep the thought in your brain.
b. Look for clues that may help you notice that you've jumped off topic, like citizens looking confused, someone saying, "What?," or the conversation suddenly stopping. If this happens, you can quickly say something like: "Oh, sorry, I spaced out!"
c. Try to set a goal for yourself that will help you stay focused so you can add comments and questions that are about the topic. For example: "I'll listen to what they're talking about and try to think of a question I can ask."

Power #5: The **Cranium Coach** power helps remind you to **use your self-talk** to tell yourself you've done well using new strategies.

- You can tell you've done this today when you can say to yourself:
"I'm able to have conversations in which I don't jump off track so often, and citizens appear to be enjoying themselves when we're talking or being together at school."

CHAPTER 3 © 2012 SOCIAL THINKING PUBLISHING

Stop! Un-Wonderer is invading your brain!
Use Superflex's Very Cool Five-Step Power Plan to defeat this Unthinkable.

Power #1: **The Decider** power helps you to **stop, describe,** and **decide** the powers of the Unthinkable.

Un-Wonderer

- **Un-Wonderer** takes away people's ability to ask questions that show interest in learning about another person (Social Wonder questions). This Unthinkable instead gets people to only ask about facts that are interesting to the person asking the question (World Wonder questions) or to ask no questions at all!

Power #2: **The Social Detective** power helps you to **observe** the situation and the people in the situation.

- Your Social Detective notices that when people are being friendly, they try and show interest in others they talk to. When people ask questions that show they're trying to get to know what another citizen has been doing or likes to do or think about, these types of questions are called Social Wonder questions. A good example is, "Did you have a good weekend?"
- When people ask World Wonder questions to learn about certain facts, the citizens who are asked the question may think that the person asking isn't really interested in them. But really the questioner is only interested in trying to learn more information to help the questioner become smarter. An example of a World Wonder question is asking someone who is about to take a trip what kind of plane he's flying on.

Power #3: **The Brakester** power helps you to **stop** and **think** to discover the hidden rules.

- If Un-Wonderer is in a citizen's brain so the person only asks World Wonder questions, the people being asked the questions may feel uncomfortable.

Power #4: **The Flex Do-Body** power helps you to **use flexible thinking** to choose strategies to use **to do** what's expected.

a. Learn more about different types of questions so you get better at learning how to ask Social Wonder questions and mostly avoid asking World Wonder questions.
b. If you know you'll be hanging out with a person you want to appear friendly to, try to think about a few Social Wonder questions ahead of time.
c. Practice asking three Social Wonder questions with different family members.

Power #5: **The Cranium Coach** power helps remind you to **use your self-talk** to tell yourself you've done well using new strategies.

- You can tell you've done this today when you can say to yourself:
"I notice I'm doing more social wondering about others and asking more questions about these wonders. I notice that others are more excited to keep talking to me and are asking me Social Wonder questions."

Stop! *WasFunnyOnce* is invading your brain!
Use Superflex's Very Cool Five-Step Power Plan to defeat this Unthinkable.

WasFunnyOnce

Power #1: **The Decider** power helps you to **stop, describe,** and **decide** the powers of the Unthinkable.

- **WasFunnyOnce** gets people to use humor at the wrong time, wrong place, or with the wrong person.

Power #2: **The Social Detective** power helps you to **observe** the situation and the people in the situation.

- Your Social Detective observes whether the time is right for humor. Some people are really good about figuring this out but many citizens can find it hard to know when and how to use humor.

Power #3: **The Brakester** power helps you to **stop** and **think** to discover the hidden rules.

- If citizens use humor, it's super important that they observe if they're telling the joke to the right person, in the right place, and at the right time. The rules about this are pretty complicated. In the classroom, the hidden rule is that if you're not sure it's a good time to joke around, it probably isn't!
- Another important hidden rule is not to think that people laughing when you do something means they're laughing with you! They may be laughing because you made them uncomfortable or may be laughing at you because they can't believe you just did or said that in a classroom.
- One more hidden rule: If you've told a friend a joke once, don't try that same joke again with the same person. That's why this Unthinkable is called WasFunnyOnce!

Power #4: **The Flex Do-Body** power helps you to **use flexible thinking** to choose strategies to use **to do** what's expected.

a. If you think you're funny and good at humor, ask someone who you trust, like a parent or a teacher who sees you around other kids, to honestly tell you if you're good at using humor. If the answer is no, work with adults to help you learn more about humor.
b. Learn about this by thinking about what you want to do or say and decide if it's the right time, right place, and with the right person.
c. Become a humor detective and try to observe and notice how students your age use humor. What kind of jokes do they use? Who are they joking with?

Power #5: **The Cranium Coach** power helps remind you to **use your self-talk** to tell yourself you've done well using new strategies.

- You can tell you've done this today when you can say to yourself:
"I'm noticing ways that others use humor and seeing some small successes with my humor among my friends or family."

THE ORIGINAL TEAM OF UNTHINKABLES: WASFUNNYONCE

CHAPTER 3 © 2012 SOCIAL THINKING PUBLISHING

Stop! *Worry Wall* is invading your brain!
Use Superflex's Very Cool Five-Step Power Plan to defeat this Unthinkable.

Power #1: **The Decider** power helps you to **stop, describe,** and **decide** the powers of the Unthinkable.

- **Worry Wall** makes people worry too much and see all worries as big worries. Worry Wall is best friends with the new Unthinkable Emotion Commotion who gets people to focus on their negative emotions.

Power #2: The Social Detective power helps you to **observe** the situation and the people in the situation.

Worry Wall

- Your Social Detective notices that everyone has some worries or fears, but some citizens seem to have a lot more of these feelings than others. Your detective can help you notice that the size of the worry or fear you have is related to how big you think a problem is or might be.

Power #3: The Brakester power helps you to **stop** and **think** to discover the hidden rules.

- It's very important for citizens to spend the time to stop and think about what's worrying them. They need to learn to figure out the difference between a very big, real problem and a small problem or glitch, which will help them learn to let go of their worries or fears.

Power #4: The Flex Do-Body power helps you to **use flexible thinking** to choose strategies to use **to do** what's expected.

a. Talk to a counselor, therapist, or parent when your brain feels like it's stuck on being worried or is filled with fear a lot of the time.
b. When you work with an adult, here are some ways to work on learning about your worrying:
   - Make a list of what makes you the most worried or fearful and of activities that keep you calm.
   - Create a worry scale where you can list your worries and fears from being a size 1 to a size 5. Chart the things from your lists on this scale.
   - Work with your therapist or counselor to try to understand if size 3, 4, and 5 worries are real problems or whether your brain is making them feel bigger than the problems actually are.
c. This learning takes time. You'll learn to worry less if you let yourself have the time to work on this.

Power #5: The Cranium Coach power helps remind you to **use your self-talk** to tell yourself you've done well using new strategies.

- You can tell you've done this today when you can say to yourself:
"I'm doing a good job taking the time to learn about my brain and to find out how to calm down some of the worries I have that are bigger than the actual problems."

CHAPTER 4

Presenting 82 New Unthinkables

This chapter introduces new Unthinkables created by many Social Town citizens of all ages. To learn more about how these Unthinkables came to be, the organization of the chapter, the Very Cool Five-Step Power Plan, and more, see chapters 1 and 2. For expanded teacher materials about many of these Unthinkables and for the image files for each of the chapter's illustrations, see the CD.

Stop! Queen of Wacky Questions
is invading your brain!
Use Superflex's Very Cool Five-Step Power Plan to defeat this Unthinkable.

Power #1: The Decider power helps you to **stop, describe,** and **decide** the powers of the Unthinkable.

- **Queen of Wacky Questions** gets people to forget the hidden rules about questions. She can make people ask questions they already know the answers to, questions that aren't about the topic being talked about, or just too many questions.

Power #2: The Social Detective power helps you to **observe** the situation and the people in the situation.

- Your Social Detective sees that when citizens talk with each other, they mostly add small thoughts about the topic and ask some questions to find out more. Citizens ask each other World Wonder questions and Social Wonder questions.
- World Wonder questions ask about facts or details that aren't about a person. Social Wonder questions ask for details about a person. Citizens seem to especially enjoy being asked Social Wonder questions.

Queen of Wacky Questions

Power #3: The Brakester power helps you to **stop** and **think** to discover the hidden rules.

- Conversations aren't always simple but they're for everyone to enjoy. People are expected to find out information from others by asking questions, though not ones they already know the answers to. A conversation usually has a good balance of talking time between people.

Power #4: The Flex Do-Body power helps you to **use flexible thinking** to choose strategies to use **to do** what's expected.

a. With help from your teacher or parent, learn more about asking questions. You can practice asking Social Wonder questions.
b. Before you ask a question, stop and ask yourself if you already know the answer. If you do, ask a different question. Also, ask yourself if the question is related to the topic.
c. If Queen of Wacky Questions often gets you to ask a lot of questions, give yourself a goal. For example: "I'll only ask three questions when I talk to my friend."

Power #5: The Cranium Coach power helps remind you to **use your self-talk** to tell yourself you've done well using new strategies.

- You can tell you've done this today when you can say to yourself:
"I think more about my questions when I talk with others. I notice that I stay on topic more during conversations and learn more about others."

Stop! Attention Eater is invading your brain!
Use Superflex's Very Cool Five-Step Power Plan to defeat this Unthinkable.

Power #1: **The Decider** power helps you to **stop, describe,** and **decide** the powers of the Unthinkable.

- **Attention Eater** makes people hungry for attention, often when they feel someone else is getting more attention than they are. Attention Eater makes people want to eat up all the attention.
- Attention Eater can sometimes get powerful enough to get a person to grab attention by doing really unexpected behaviors and not notice that this can make others mad!

Attention Eater

Power #2: **The Social Detective** power helps you to **observe** the situation and the people in the situation.

- Your Social Detective observes who is getting attention in a situation and for what reasons. When you do things that make citizens upset and they give you attention but seem grumpy or mad at you at the same time, this is called receiving "negative attention." Attention Eater tries to convince people that negative attention is good because it makes everyone unhappy.

Power #3: **The Brakester** power helps you to **stop** and **think** to discover the hidden rules.

- All citizens like some level of attention. If someone is getting attention, that person may become frustrated if someone else comes up and tries to take the attention away. Learning to pay attention to others and allowing others to be given attention when you're not getting any is considered a friendly or thoughtful thing to do.

Power #4: **The Flex Do-Body** power helps you to **use flexible thinking** to choose strategies to use **to do** what's expected.

- a. Observe others and know that you can let teachers and other students share attention with each other.
- b. If Attention Eater gets you to do things you know are against the rules to get attention, remember how frustrating it is when people are mad at you or aren't nice to you when they pay you all this attention.
- c. Notice what's expected, and watch your actions to try and decrease the number of times you get attention for doing unexpected behavior in specific situations.

Power #5: **The Cranium Coach** power helps remind you to **use your self-talk** to tell yourself you've done well using new strategies.

- You can tell you've done this today when you can say to yourself:
"I've learned to feel good when others receive attention, and I'm learning to seek attention for doing what's expected."

Stop! *Copy Cat* is invading your brain!

- **Copy Cat** makes people use their body or voice to imitate other people, which is sure to annoy those people. Copy Cat sometimes teams up with WasFunnyOnce.

To do what's expected, use these Superflex strategies:

a. Use self-talk: "My classmates get frustrated or annoyed with me if I copy their behavior, their words, or their tone of voice. They might like it better if I try to stay connected by adding my thoughts and words."

b. Stop and think with your eyes to see what the other group members are doing. Are they just standing and talking? Are they sitting and eating? To stay connected, try to take part in the activity that they're doing.

c. If Copy Cat gets in your brain and wants you to repeat what others are saying or their tone of voice, defeat this Unthinkable by listening to what they're talking about and adding your own thoughts to the discussion rather than copying someone else. Notice if Copy Cat and WasFunnyOnce both get in your brain and work together to make you think that copying others' behavior is funny and convince you that other people think this is funny. If this happens, beware! People may laugh at first but they get annoyed really quickly when they're being mimicked. People often laugh even when they're getting irritated! Don't trust that just because people are laughing that they like what you're doing. If they laugh and then avoid being with you, your humor definitely wasn't as funny as WasFunnyOnce was trying to make you think it was!

Copy Cat

Stop! *Get in Trouble Man* is invading your brain!

- **Get in Trouble Man** makes students in class get in trouble by doing unexpected behaviors. This Unthinkable gets students to think they're so cute or clever that they can convince the teacher that someone else did the unexpected behavior so they don't get in trouble.

- Get in Trouble Man also likes to hang out with WasFunnyOnce and Attention Eater to get students to do silly unexpected things in class to get attention — like try to tell a joke in the middle of a teacher's lesson, make fun of the teacher, or pull a prank on someone in class.

a. Use your Social Detective powers to look for "silly moment" clues to help you only use your humor at the right time and place and around the right people while in class. These clues include:
    ◆ The teacher smiles and laughs while making a funny comment about the lesson or topic.
    ◆ The other students are laughing with the teacher.
    ◆ The teacher's body looks relaxed and friendly.

b. Look at a Social Behavior Map about what's expected for learning in a classroom and notice how many of these behaviours you're using. Your teacher can help with this. When you focus on doing expected behaviors in different situations in your class, it's likely the teacher thinks you're a helpful member of the classroom.

c. When you're tempted to do something unexpected, use your inner coach to help you get through the moment. "I know if I keep doing what's expected, my teacher and classmates will have good thoughts about me and I'll learn the information my teacher needs to teach me."

d. If you lose control and do something unexpected, be honest and let the teacher know it was you. That way, your classmates won't get angry with you for making up a lie and blaming them.

Get in Trouble Man

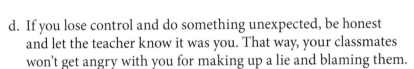

Stop! The Whiner is invading your brain!

Powers of this Unthinkable

*   **The Whiner** gets a person's voice to suddenly become high pitched, which makes people who are nearby want to cover their ears. The Whiner then gets the person to start to complain about everything and not do what's expected.

To do what's expected, use these Superflex strategies:

a. Take a deep breath and talk calmly in your own relaxed tone of voice. If you're not sure what your voice sounds like when it's relaxed versus when it's "whining," tape record both types of voice with a teacher or parent. Listen to the recordings to help you hear the difference.

b. Use self-talk: "This might not be what I wanted to do right now, but I can make the best of it."

c. Remember that others don't want to help you when you use a whiny voice.

The Whiner

Stop! Blurt Out Blue is invading your brain!
Use Superflex's Very Cool Five-Step Power Plan to defeat this Unthinkable.

Power #1: **The Decider** power helps you to **stop, describe,** and **decide** the powers of the Unthinkable.

- **Blurt Out Blue** gets people to shout out answers to questions or make comments when it's not their turn. He often teams up with Volume Volumizer to make people talk too loud when they blurt.

Power #2: **The Social Detective** power helps you to **observe** the situation and the people in the situation.

Blurt Out Blue

- During a class discussion, your Social Detective helps you think with your eyes and see which student the teacher is talking to or appears to be thinking about.
- If you don't think with your eyes to figure out who is talking to whom, Blurt Out Blue is more likely to get you to blurt — meaning you speak without paying attention to whether you're welcome to speak at that time or not!

Power #3: **The Brakester** power helps you to **stop** and **think** to discover the hidden rules.

- In classrooms, students are expected to have thoughts about the topics being discussed. What's difficult for students is figuring out when it's a good time to say these out loud and when to try and keep the thoughts in their head. If one citizen keeps blurting out, citizens can get frustrated and think the blurter is being selfish by not allowing other people to have time to speak.

Power #4: **The Flex Do-Body** power helps you to **use flexible thinking** to choose strategies to use **to do** what's expected.

a. Think with your eyes and figure out if you should say what you're thinking.
b. If you've raised your hand to speak, look to see if the teacher is looking at you and about to call on you. If not, keep the thought in your head or write it in your thought journal to remember..
c. During discussions in which everyone is jumping in to speak, watch the speaker to see when that citizen will be done talking. Be ready to speak next.

Power #5: **The Cranium Coach** power helps remind you to **use your self-talk** to tell yourself you've done well using new strategies.

- You can tell you've done this today when you can say to yourself:
"No one said I was blurting or that it wasn't my turn to talk. I'm also starting to know when it's a good time for me to speak!"

Stop! **Boastful Bore** is invading your brain!

Use Superflex's Very Cool Five-Step Power Plan to defeat this Unthinkable.

Power #1: **The Decider** power helps you to **stop, describe, and decide** the powers of the Unthinkable.

- **Boastful Bore** makes people brag about themselves and not think about how their comments make others feel.

Power #2: **The Social Detective** power helps you to **observe** the situation and the people in the situation.

- Your Social Detective observes that it can get really annoying if people talk all the time about how smart they are or how well they've done. You should be proud of who you are and what you do, but if that's all you talk about, other people can get frustrated with you and think you aren't interested in them.

Power #3: **The Brakester** power helps you to **stop** and **think** to discover the hidden rules.

- People are expected to ask others questions to find out what they're doing and what they've done. Citizens are also supposed to try not to make anyone else feel bad.

Boastful Bore

Power #4: **The Flex Do-Body** power helps you to **use flexible thinking** to choose strategies to use **to do** what's expected.

a. Think about how your comments make other people feel.
b. Ask other people about what they've done or what they're doing.
c. If you know someone hasn't done well on a project or test and you have, keep your thoughts about your success in your head so you don't sound boastful!
d. Remember that helping your friends and siblings to feel good about who they are helps them and others to feel good about you.
e. When you feel proud of what you've done, tell yourself that you're proud of you!

Power #5: **The Cranium Coach** power helps remind you to **use your self-talk** to tell yourself you've done well using new strategies.

- You can tell you've done this today when you can say to yourself:
  "I've held my boastful thoughts in my head and have spent time showing interest in others."

Stop! *First Fighter* is invading your brain!
Use Superflex's Very Cool Five-Step Power Plan to defeat this Unthinkable.

Power #1: **The Decider** power helps you to **stop, describe,** and **decide** the powers of the Unthinkable.

- **First Fighter** makes people think they need to be first in line all the time and gets them really upset when they're not.

Power #2: **The Social Detective** power helps you to **observe** the situation and the people in the situation.

- Your Social Detective sees that students in the room mostly line up in a calm way. Even when they aren't first in line, they just get into the line and keep their bodies relaxed and use expected words.

Power #3: **The Brakester** power helps you to **stop** and **think** to discover the hidden rules.

- Everybody has to get into lines. Teachers often ask students to get in line when they change from one activity to the next.
- People are expected to stay calm wherever they are in line. Whether they're first, fifth, or last in line, they'll still end up in the same place with everyone else.

First Fighter

Power #4: **The Flex Do-Body** power helps you to **use flexible thinking** to choose strategies to use **to do** what's expected.

a. Stop and think about the size of the problem: "It's not a big deal to be in the middle or at the end of the line sometimes. I'll get to the same place with everyone else."
b. Play a guessing game in your head of what number you'll be in line each day in which you plan to be in a different spot each day.
c. Stop, look, and ask yourself: "How fast or slow are students walking toward the line?" "Are they crying and yelling when they aren't first in line?" Then try to have yourself match the behavior of your peers as you line up.
d. Practice keeping your reactions small and your body calm when you aren't first in line. Take some deep breaths when it's line-up time. Say to yourself, "Oh well, maybe I'll be first another day."

Power #5: **The Cranium Coach** power helps remind you to **use your self-talk** to tell yourself you've done well using new strategies.

- You can tell you've done this today when you can say to yourself:
"I can stay calm wherever I am in line!

Stop! Miss Turn Taker is invading your brain!

Powers of this Unthinkable

- **Miss Turn Taker** gets a person to take other people's turns away from them and to insist that he or she is the one to go first. This Unthinkable can also get a person to push or get physical with others to be able to take a turn ahead of everyone else. For example, if citizens are in line to go down a slide, Miss Turn Taker might get a person to push someone who is ahead out of the way to be able to go next.

To do what's expected, use these Superflex strategies:

a. Think to yourself: "Maybe I should let all these people go because I've had a turn." and "Even if I don't get to go first, I'll still get food in the lunch line or still get to have a turn in the game."

b. Think about the size of the problem. Remind yourself that this is a tiny problem and that the world won't end if you don't get to go first. If you're at recess and notice yourself becoming frustrated because you have to wait your turn on the playground equipment, take a breath and tell yourself: "I'll get a turn soon. Everyone has to wait just like me."

Miss Turn Taker

Stop, Noodle Dude is invading your brain!

Powers of this Unthinkable

- There really is such a thing as being TOO flexible. **Noodle Dude** loves to make an appearance around game time and activities when there are turns to be taken or choices to be made. Noodle Dude makes it seem like a person doesn't care what gets decided and wants everyone else to make the decisions! Whatever, Dude.

To do what's expected, use these Superflex strategies:

a. Use the Idea + Choice formula to make a choice. Ask yourself: "What are the positives and negatives for my different ideas?" Then rank the ideas and make a choice now, choosing the one that sounds the best.

Noodle Dude

b. Remember that because others may add more ideas, your idea may not be chosen. That's okay because sharing your idea shows the group that you're thinking about them.

c. Use the Just Make a Choice approach: If you can't come up with a choice on your own and your friends have given their own ideas, go with the one that sounds best to you. You can say something like, "I like Jamy's idea; I'd like to do that."

d. Think about the hidden rules for adding ideas to the group. When you take part in a game or activity with others, everyone listens to what others suggest and shares their own ideas. This is a way people show they're thinking about others in a group. Sometimes people may not share an idea. If this happens all the time, group members can feel like you're not helping the group. They may feel like they have to do all the work or wonder if you want to be in the group at all. So jump in and try to share a new idea or agree with one that was already suggested.

e. If you can guess ahead of time what your group will be doing — like playing a game, deciding where you want to go eat, or picking an activity — have some ideas in mind before the discussion comes up so you're ready to add your ideas.

Stop! *Time Racer* is invading your brain!

Powers of this Unthinkable

- **Time Racer** gets people's brains to worry about needing to do schoolwork too fast. This Unthinkable makes people want to be done first, no matter what! This usually leads to messy work, careless mistakes, and an unhappy teacher and student.

To do what's expected, use these Superflex strategies:

a. Use self-talk: "There's almost never a prize for finishing first." "How does my teacher expect me to do this work?" "I should take my time so I can do my best work and feel really good about my work."

b. Think with your eyes: Look around and see that no one is racing you to get done first.

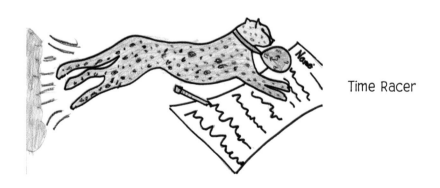

Time Racer

Stop! Danger Dave is invading your brain!
Use Superflex's Very Cool Five-Step Power Plan to defeat this Unthinkable.

Power #1: **The Decider** power helps you to **stop, describe,** and **decide** the powers of the Unthinkable.

- When **Danger Dave** is around, people forget to notice if things are safe or not, which can cause harm to them or others. Danger Dave might make people jump on unsafe things, run quickly around a corner without looking, or swing their arms around without noticing there's a friend right there who might get hit.

Danger Dave

Power #2: **The Social Detective** power helps you to **observe** the situation and the people in the situation.

- Your Social Detective observes where you are and what's expected in that location. Usually, citizens' bodies are pretty calm inside schools, homes, and most Social Town places. The main reason for calmer bodies out in Social Town is safety so citizens don't get hurt or feel uncomfortable about the behavior of others.

Power #3: **The Brakester** power helps you to **stop** and **think** to discover the hidden rules.

- It's expected that citizens use their Social Detective powers to think about how to act in different situations to keep others feeling safe and comfortable.

Power #4: **The Flex Do-Body** power helps you to **use flexible thinking** to choose strategies to use **to do** what's expected.

a. Do a safety check: Stop, look, and ask yourself: "Could I fall? Could I get hurt? Could I bump into or hurt someone? What's expected here?"
b. Use your detective powers to see if you notice others doing the behavior. Also try to think about how people are acting so that you can try to match the behaviors.
c. Create a list with a teacher or an adult about where big movements like running and jumping are expected, like during recess or P.E.
d. If your brain and body think a lot about moving around, your teacher or parent can talk to an occupational therapist for help with figuring out some strategies that you can use to calm your body.

Power #5: **The Cranium Coach** power helps remind you to **use your self-talk** to tell yourself you've done well using new strategies.

- You can tell you've done this today when you can say to yourself:
"I've learned to keep my body calm and notice that others around me feel comfortable."

stop! Fear Releaser is invading your brain!
Use Superflex's Very Cool Five-Step Power Plan to defeat this Unthinkable.

Power #1: **The Decider** power helps you to **stop, describe,** and **decide** the powers of the Unthinkable.

- **Fear Releaser** makes people fearful of things that aren't likely to happen or could never happen. These fears sometimes become so strong that they prevent people from doing things, no matter how much they want to do them.

Fear Releaser

Power #2: **The Social Detective** power helps you to **observe** the situation and the people in the situation.

- Use your Social Detective powers to observe when you start to show signs of worry and fear (an adult can help you notice the signs). Detect how little worries or fears come up for other citizens daily and how they manage those fears.

Power #3: **The Brakester** power helps you to **stop** and **think** to discover the hidden rules.

- It's expected that people take control of their unrealistic fears so that they can stay focused on the here and now.

Power #4: **The Flex Do-Body** power helps you to **use flexible thinking** to choose strategies to use **to do** what's expected.

a. If you start to feel fearful, ask yourself: Is this a real fear based on realistic thoughts or an unrealistic fear caused by Fear Releaser? A real fear is about a pretty big problem. An example is if other students threaten to hurt you after school. If something like this happens, get help from an adult right away! An unrealistic fear changes your thinking so you worry about things that aren't likely to happen or would never happen. An example is thinking, "I'll never pass this class no matter what I do."

b. Notice when your thoughts or body begin to react to a fear and use your strategies to help yourself stay calm while you work through your fear. This may take help at first from your school team and family.

c. Use your inner coach to help keep your thoughts positive. For example: "I can fight this fear. I've done it before and I know ways to do this."

d. Try thinking of something you enjoy or that makes you feel calm.

Power #5: **The Cranium Coach** power helps remind you to **use your self-talk** to tell yourself you've done well using new strategies.

- You can tell you've done this today when you can say to yourself:
"I feel calmer about myself and notice that I'm challenging myself to do things that I once thought were too hard or scary."

Stop! *Emotion Commotion* is invading your brain!
Use Superflex's Very Cool Five-Step Power Plan to defeat this Unthinkable.

Power #1: **The Decider** power helps you to **stop, describe,** and **decide** the powers of the Unthinkable.

- **Emotion Commotion** makes people focus too much on their emotions, especially when they feel sad, mad, or upset. When this happens, they can't focus on anything else. Emotion Commotion is the best friend of Worry Wall.

Power #2: **The Social Detective** power helps you to **observe** the situation and the people in the situation.

- Your Super Detective notices that all citizens have many different types of feelings inside, also called emotions, during each day. Emotions aren't a problem — they're part of who people are as humans. What can be a problem is if Emotion Commotion gets your emotions stuck so much on feeling blah, yucky, or mad that it's hard for you to feel like there's anything good going on in your life.

Emotion Commotion

Power #3: **The Brakester** power helps you to **stop** and **think** to discover the hidden rules.

- It's not always easy for citizens to figure out how they feel, and it's even harder sometimes to know why they feel the way they do. But people know that the way they feel can affect how they act with other people. When Emotion Commotion gets stuck in citizen' brains, they need help from an adult who can guide them to learn more about their emotions!

Power #4: **The Flex Do-Body** power helps you to **use flexible thinking** to choose strategies to use **to do** what's expected.

a. When your emotions feel in commotion, ask for a break from what you're doing to help yourself calm down.
b. Once you calm down a little, try to figure out what's making you feel so upset. To be more aware of how you feel, use strategies from the Thinkable Rainbow Girl.
c. Ask for help from an adult if you're asked to do something that you feel is too hard or just too confusing.
d. Remember, that citizens' emotions change throughout a day and you probably won't feel this way for much longer.

Power #5: **The Cranium Coach** power helps remind you to **use your self-talk** to tell yourself you've done well using new strategies.

- You can tell you've done this today when you can say to yourself:
"I did a good job learning about my emotions today and I'm slowly learning how I can help myself feel better even in a bad situation!"

Emotion Commotion, Hurtful Harry, Icky Vicky, Mood Keeper, Past Willy, and Rainstorm are all siblings! Superflex has the same powers to defeat them!

Stop! Hurtful Harry is invading your brain!

Powers of this Unthinkable

- **Hurtful Harry** usually shows up when a person is angry or frustrated. He tries to make that person hurt someone else by scratching, biting, hitting, or kicking that person. He often teams up with Glassman.

To do what's expected, use these Superflex strategies:

a. Walk away from what or who is making you mad. If you can't do this on your own, tell an adult you're mad and ask for help in getting calm.

b. Once you're calm again, ask your teacher or another adult for some extra quiet time. This can help you get stronger to stay calm. You can ask the adult to help you work through the problem that made you get so angry.
   - Use calming strategies. These are some you can use:
   - STAR: Stop, Take a deep breath, And, Relax.
   - Take deep breaths, breathing in through your nose and out through your mouth.
   - Count to 10.

Hurtful Harry

c. As you learn to calm down after you get angry, start to figure out what makes you angry.
   - When you do that, you can learn to remove yourself from that type of situation sooner.
   - Look at the size of the problem for the times you know you get angry. Tip: Look at the Superflex strategies that show ways to defeat Glassman. Hurtful Harry and Glassman are best friends and feed off each other's powers!

Stop! Icky Vicky is invading your brain!

Powers of this Unthinkable

- **Icky Vicky** makes people feel bad about themselves. When Icky Vicky has her way, people feel sad and grumpy and then other people think they don't want to hang out. That's how Icky Vicky stops people from making friends.

To do what's expected, use these Superflex strategies:

a. One of the ways that can make you feel a bit better is if people come over to talk to you and show interest in you. Practice looking and acting more "approachable." (This means you have your head up and an okay to pleasant look on your face. You look as if you want to join in with what other people are doing or say hi when you pass them.)

b. If you can do this, it's more likely people will come to talk to you. It's a well-known fact that if you look like you want to avoid people, they'll try and stay away from you. And if people stay away from you, it may make you feel even worse!

c. Learn more about what feels hard for you. Make a plan with a trusted teacher, parent, or friend to help you learn one little thing each day to help you feel better about the things you believe are harder for you.

Icky Vicky

Stop! Mood Keeper is invading your brain!

Powers of this Unthinkable

- **Mood Keeper** makes people stay in a bad mood or have a hard time moving out of a bad mood.

To do what's expected, use these Superflex strategies:

- To defeat Mood Keeper, you can use almost all of the same strategies as for Emotion Commotion, Icky Vicky, and Rainstorm. Here's information about some of these strategies:

a. Think of happy thoughts that can make you feel better.

b. Learn ways that help you know how you feel and what you can do, wherever you are, to help you feel at least okay. That

Mood Keeper

will help you do your best in what's happening at that time. Talk to your teacher or another adult you trust for help with this. Sometimes getting exercise or taking a break from something that seems very hard can help you move from a more negative mood to more of an okay or positive mood.

c. Find what you're good at and work at recognizing those "smarts" to make yourself feel better about the many things you do well.

Stop! Past Willy is invading your brain!

Powers of this Unthinkable

- **Past Willy** gets a person to carry around heavy — scary or bad — memories and thoughts about what happened in the person's life before.

To do what's expected, use these Superflex strategies:

a. Imagine the heavy thoughts are being carried in a suitcase or luggage in your mind. Learn to lighten the load by dumping off your brain's "luggage" or "suitcase" in one place before you can focus on working on what you need to do in that moment in another place.

b. Talk to your teacher or parent about it when your mind feels heavy with thoughts and memories. Then they can help to teach you more ways and places for dropping off your luggage.

Past Willy

c. Use your inner coach to help: "I notice I'm doing a good job keeping Past Willy out of my mind when I'm able to stop thinking about the heavy thoughts in my mind and I'm able to focus on being with other people or doing my classwork. This way I can build new happier and lighter memories."

Stop! Rainstorm is invading your brain!

Powers of this Unthinkable

- **Rainstorm** makes people gloomy and sad and may stay around for a long time.

To do what's expected, use these Superflex strategies:

a. When your brain gets stuck on upset, sometimes being in the place you are can make you feel even more upset. Getting somewhere where it's easier for you to calm down is important. At home or school, find a special place that makes you feel better and helps you stop Rainstorm. For example, some students like being in the library, some like spending extra time in the classroom during some breaks in the school day, and others like being able to find a different quiet place at school where they can get away from everything going on around them!

b. Work at learning to think about some positive things in your day and life. You may want to bring in a picture book of people, pets, or things that make you feel good to remind yourself of them.

c. If you feel you don't have enough people your own age to talk to at school, talk to a teacher or counselor about this. They can help make a plan to begin to have other students your age to be with you at different times during the day.

Rainstorm

Stop! Prickly Pete the Porcupine is invading your brain!

Powers of this Unthinkable

- **Prickly Pete the Porcupine** gets people to look grumpy and unapproachable to others.

To do what's expected, use these Superflex strategies:

a. Ask yourself: "How will it look to others if you seem angry or grumpy or you snap at someone with your words?"

Prickly Pete the Porcupine

b. Figure out the person's reason for coming up to you, their plan. Most people approach you for a friendly reason like saying hi, to chat, to play, or maybe to ask for your help on something. These are all things citizens do to show they're thinking about someone else. If you can start to see all the positive interactions you can have with people, you can start to change your grumpy thinking ("Grr… they're coming over to just bother me") to more positive self-talk ("Hey, they were friendly the last time we talked and it was nice"). This will make it a little easier to wipe the grumpy look away.

c. If you're feeling nervous or uncomfortable, explain your situation: "I'm just feeling a little stressed/busy/nervous…" or "I have _____ going on/coming up…" This is a better choice than ignoring people or acting in a way that makes them think you're mad at them. Each person has felt nervous or stressed at times and can understand if you tell them that's how you're feeling. It's also very possible that the other person feels the same way.

Stop! The Enforcer is invading your brain!
Use Superflex's Very Cool Five-Step Power Plan to defeat this Unthinkable.

The Enforcer

Power #1: The **Decider** power helps you to **stop, describe,** and **decide** the powers of the Unthinkable.

- **The Enforcer** gets people to try to make everybody follow all the rules.

Power #2: The **Social Detective** power helps you to **observe** the situation and the people in the situation.

- Your Social Detective sees that citizens have all types of rules, including for playing games. A rule gives people a guide for what to do or how to behave.
- When you play a game, rules are often flexible. This means the rules can change a bit and the game can still be played. Your Social Detective has to watch out for The Enforcer who can make you forget that playing games is all about having fun and being flexible.

Power #3: The **Brakester** power helps you to **stop** and **think** to discover the hidden rules.

- Here are some of the expected ways to deal with rules when citizens play games:
  - When playing a new game, the rules can be said out loud once for everyone to hear. If one player thinks someone isn't following the rules exactly, the players have to decide how big a problem this is and what to do.
  - If most players decide to change the rules a little and the game can still be played well, all players are expected to go along with the changes.

Power #4: The **Flex Do-Body** power helps you to **use flexible thinking** to choose strategies to use **to do** what's expected.

a. Remember the purpose of playing games is to enjoy the people you're with while doing an activity.
b. Avoid telling the rules to people when they already know them unless they ask.
c. Practice being a flexible thinker by not getting upset if the rules change a little and aren't exactly what you think they should be.
d. If some players are upset about rule changes and a teacher is nearby, ask for help to work it out.

Power #5: The **Cranium Coach** power helps remind you to **use your self-talk** to tell yourself you've done well using new strategies.

- You can tell you've done this today when you can say to yourself:
  "I started to use my flexible brain and thought about enjoying the game with other people. This means I can stop focusing on the rules and instead focus on how we all get along together."

Stop! Holiday Boulder is invading your brain!

Powers of this Unthinkable

- **Holiday Boulder,** who is Rock Brain's cousin, looks for people's brains during the holidays. This Unthinkable gets people stuck on ALL their holiday traditions and won't let any new plans change those traditions.

  Holiday Boulder often teams up with Glassman to make people react too strongly whenever holiday plans are even talked about.

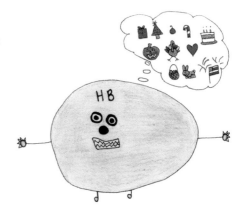

Holiday Boulder

To do what's expected, use these Superflex strategies:

a. Use self-talk to help you think more positively. Here are some examples:
   - "Being part of a family means that I might not always get my way and that's okay. Sometimes because we're part of a family we have to change our thinking to keep others feeling good."
   - "I can be flexible and try something new with my family. It might be fun!"
   - "Even if the holiday plans I would like are different, my family will still be together and that makes me happy."

b. Once you create a new holiday memory, store it in a Holiday Memories file in your brain. Then you can pull up the file when any new holiday changes start to upset you. You'll remember that you had a nice time when the plans changed last time. This will make it easier to change your plans in the future.

c. Think about how changing a holiday plan is a small problem when compared to an "earthquake" (huge) problem. Think about matching the problem with a small reaction like saying, "Okay, that sounds okay" when your parents make different holiday plans.

Stop! Justice Buster is invading your brain!

Powers of this Unthinkable

- **Justice Buster** makes people forget about having fun and gets them to only worry about making sure everything is fair.

To do what's expected, use these Superflex strategies:

Justice Buster

a. Think about the feelings of other citizens — imagine how others feel when all the fun is ruined by one person demanding a fair share.

Stop! *Rule Police* are invading your brain!

Rule Police

Powers of this Unthinkable

- **Rule Police** make people think that it's their job to remind others about even the smallest rules. When the Rule Police are around, people believe that there's only one right way to do something and that they have to correct others. They often don't see that others find this behavior very annoying.

To do what's expected, use these Superflex strategies:

a. Use self-talk: "Not everyone likes to be told how to do something or what to do."

b. Remind yourself that all citizens are responsible for their own actions and choices. Your job isn't to be the Rule Police.

Stop! *Time Keeper* is invading your brain!

Time Keeper

Powers of this Unthinkable

- **Time Keeper** makes people get stuck on following a schedule EXACTLY, to the minute. Time Keeper may make people ask things like, "How many more do I have to do before I get to play?" or "How long will this take?"

You'll notice that Time Keeper looks both worried and angry. This is because in addition to trying to make someone stuck on the times in a schedule, Time Keeper tries to make people worry, get angry, and even feel "stressed out." Time Keeper is closely related to Rock Brain and often teams up with Worry Wall and Glassman.

To do what's expected, use these Superflex strategies:

a. Understand that the adult you're with will make sure that the schedule is followed but not to the exact minute. If there will be a big schedule change, this adult will probably let you know before Time Keeper starts messing with you.

b. Think: "It's okay if the clock says it's time for_____; people don't follow time exactly. I can wait patiently until I'm able to do _____ ."

c. Remember, a schedule is meant to be your friend, not something that causes you to get upset. Schedules help people know what happens next. A specific time on a schedule is just a time that's close to when the event will happen.

d. If citizens let Time Keeper get them stuck and upset about the time on a schedule, it throws everyone off schedule because they now have to take time to calm Time Keeper back down. That wasn't on the schedule! Remember that if you get upset, it may take even longer for the group and schedule to get back on track.

e. Think: "If the clock says I'm late, it's okay. I'll probably get to do it anyway."

f. Don't be like the White Rabbit in *Alice in Wonderland.* Time Keeper will make you think you need to get as upset and worried as the White Rabbit, but you really don't. Remember that being like the White Rabbit doesn't help you or anyone else.

Stop! Tiny Teacher is invading your brain!

Powers of this Unthinkable

- **Tiny Teacher** causes people to act like the teacher. This includes giving orders or directions that the teacher normally gives. Tiny Teacher says, "I get people to act like they're in charge or they're the teacher."

To do what's expected, use these Superflex strategies:

a. Remember that each citizen is only responsible for controlling his or her own behavior. If there's a possible problem with how another student is acting, the classroom teacher is the only person in charge of deciding how to help the student to change that behavior.

b. Keep in mind that not everything you see as a problem is something other citizens or even a teacher would agree is a problem!

c. Stop yourself from telling others how to act because this might cause them to feel frustrated or angry.

d. Put your thoughts in your own mind's lock box if you have the urge to tell someone else how to behave or what to do.

e. Figure out who is in charge of the group — if it isn't you, use your lock box!

f. Say to yourself: "I'm only in charge of myself. I'll let the teacher decide if she should take care of the situation I see."

g. Ask yourself: "How will the teacher feel and how will my classmates feel if I tell other students how they should behave?"

Tiny Teacher

Stop! Munchie Munchie is invading your brain!
Use Superflex's Very Cool Five-Step Power Plan to defeat this Unthinkable.

Munchie Munchie

Power #1: The Decider power helps you to **stop, describe,** and **decide** the powers of the Unthinkable.

- **Munchie Munchie** makes people have a big urge to eat something they shouldn't eat because it's unhealthy. This Unthinkable also gets people to want to snack or eat at unexpected times.

Power #2: The Social Detective power helps you to **observe** the situation and the people in the situation.

- If you feel like you just have to eat that food, use your Social Detective powers to look around to see if others are eating it too. It might not be the right time to eat. When your class or family is making food together, your Social Detective helps you know if it's an okay time to take a taste. Your teacher might say, "Everyone can have a bite now."

Power #3: The Brakester power helps you to **stop** and **think** to discover the hidden rules.

- There are usually times when citizens stop what they're doing and have something to eat. People know that their bodies need certain types of food (healthy foods) for energy and to stay healthy. People also have to learn which foods may taste good but are unhealthy or unsafe.
- Before you eat, think about whether or not a food is truly COOKED and safe to eat. Some ingredients need to cook before you can eat them — like eggs in cake batter. Unsafe foods may make you very sick if you eat them.

Power #4: The Flex Do-Body power helps you to **use flexible thinking** to choose strategies to use **to do** what's expected.

a. Think before you eat. Ask yourself: "Is everyone else having a bite?," "Is this the right time?," "Is this healthy to eat now or could it make me sick?," or "Can I wait just a little longer?"

b. Get your inner coach to help. Say to yourself: "If I don't resist, I might not get to do something like this again." If you've been reminded not to eat, you can tell yourself: "If I eat this now, people may get mad at me."

c. Shift your mind. Sometimes when Munchie Munchie gets in your head, you have to focus away from food and on something else. Even adults do this.

d. Choose a different food. Make healthier choices that make Munchie Munchie melt away.

Power #5: The Cranium Coach power helps remind you to **use your self-talk** to tell yourself you've done well using new strategies.

- You can tell you've done this today when you can say to yourself: "I've successfully used my eyes, ears, and brain to know when it's the expected time to eat AND I've used my Superflex strategies to make good choices about food!"

Stop! The Junkanator is invading your brain!

- **The Junkanator** makes people crave and eat too much junk food.

To do what's expected, use these Superflex strategies:

a. One of your Superflex powers is a special apple sensor that lets you know when you're about to eat junk food, like a candy apple. You can use that sensor to help you switch to something healthy, like an apple.

b. With your parents, come up with a Good Choice list of foods that taste good that are also healthy for you. When you're tempted to eat junk food, select a better choice from your list.

c. Trying to stay away from junk food and keeping The Junkanator out of your brain is hard. Make sure you're setting small goals that you can reach. Try switching just one junk food choice with a healthy choice one time this week and then try for two times the next week.

d. Make sure to have a healthy breakfast plan each morning. Breakfast is super important and gives you energy for the day and power to defeat The Junkanator.

The Junkanator

e. Use this story to help you use your apple sensor:

The Adventures of Emi-Flex

One day in Healthyville, a girl named Emily was eating a mac and cheese lunch. When she finished all of it, she wanted more. When she went to get more, she found a special sensor called the apple sensor hidden in the basement. The apple sensor began to talk: "I was once a strong healthy fruit until I was defeated by The Junkanator — now I'm a candy apple. To turn me back to a nutritious snack, you must defeat The Junkanator!"

Stop! Picky Peater is invading your brain!

- **Picky Peater** makes people not want to try new foods or gets them to reject foods for minor or unimportant reasons. When this Unthinkable has invaded, people want to do unexpected things with their faces or make negative comments about what others are eating.

a. Many times food companies put different brand labels on several bags or boxes but put the SAME EXACT food on the inside. When people taste the food, it's the same! If someone offers food that you like, but it's a different brand, just relax and say to yourself, "This will probably taste the same — it's no big deal."

Picky Peater

b. If someone offers you a food you've never tried or something you think you don't like, use your self-talk to go on a "food safari." This is a tradition passed down through the generations of Social Town citizens. It's also something that Superflex himself had to learn to do when asked to be flexible about trying new foods. Here's how it works:

   ◆ Picture yourself as a mighty hunter of strange and exotic foods (you could even draw a picture). You carry only the most important supplies: a fork or spoon, your tastebuds, and your flexible brain.

   ◆ Your job is to track the food (look at it), surround it (put it in your mouth), and then capture it for your stomach zoo (swallow it into your stomach).

   ◆ Have your inner coach keep reminding you, "Take a deep breath and try to remember that trying new foods is not a big problem. Remember that every food you now like was once a new food for you to try!"

c. When others are eating something that looks yucky to you, stop and think: "Does it really matter to me what other people eat?" Say to yourself: "I can think whatever I want about that food but I don't have to say it out loud."

 **Stop!** *Stick to Me Sam* is invading your brain!
Use Superflex's Very Cool Five-Step Power Plan to defeat this Unthinkable.

Stick to Me Sam

Power #1: **The Decider** power helps you to **stop, describe,** and **decide** the powers of the Unthinkable.

- **Stick to Me Sam** makes a person very upset and disappointed when a friend wants to play or talk with someone else. Stick to Me Sam also gets people to think if someone is nice to them, that person wants to be their best friend. They then may get upset when the friend doesn't want to be best friends.

Power #2: **The Social Detective** power helps you to **observe** the situation and the people in the situation.

- Your Social Detective observes that there are different levels of knowing someone, from an acquaintance to an evolving friend, a friend, and a best friend.
- A friendship can take a long time to create. It's pretty common for citizens to have several friends. If Stick to Me Sam can, he'll get you to think that friendships are confusing and complicated, but you can learn ways to help you develop friendships.

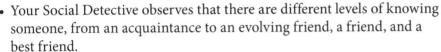 **Power #3:** **The Brakester** power helps you to **stop** and **think** to discover the hidden rules.

- It's expected that citizens remember the levels of friendship because there are rules to follow for each level. It's important that a citizen understands what level he or she is on with a friend and that both people have the same understanding. If one citizen thinks they're best friends, but the other person feels that they're evolving friends, there may be some confusion about how much time they'll spend with each other.

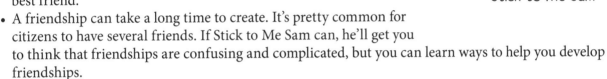 **Power #4:** **The Flex Do-Body** power helps you to **use flexible thinking** to choose strategies to use **to do** what's expected.

a. Work with your teacher or parent to learn about the different levels of friendship and the hidden rules about each level.
b. If there's someone you're friends with, remember that it's expected for friends to have other friends. This may be hard to deal with but some positive self-talk can help you get through the moment.
c. If you see a friend with someone else, use your inner coach to tell yourself that that this is a tiny problem. Try to join the group of a different friend or an evolving friend.

Power #5: **The Cranium Coach** power helps remind you to **use your self-talk** to tell yourself you've done well using new strategies.

- You can tell you've done this today when you can say to yourself:
"I can stay calm when a person I want to be with is spending time with someone else. I can find someone else to spend time with now."

Stop! Confusion Carol is invading your brain!
Use Superflex's Very Cool Five-Step Power Plan to defeat this Unthinkable.

Confusion Carol

Power #1: **The Decider** power helps you to **stop, describe,** and **decide** the powers of the Unthinkable.

- **Confusion Carol** gets people confused when they're together with others. She can get people so confused that they don't understand what others mean by what they're saying and aren't even sure about the topic.

Power #2: **The Social Detective** power helps you to **observe** the situation and the people in the situation.

- Your Social Detective notices that people often think with their eyes to make smart guesses to help them figure out social times before they react. Sometimes your social memory can help you make even smarter guesses about the situation. Your social memory is what your brain remembers about other people and social situations.

Power #3: **The Brakester** power helps you to **stop** and **think** to discover the hidden rules.

- Social times can be confusing, and citizens try to figure them out by putting together clues about the people and the events so they can act with expected behaviors. When they don't understand something, they can ask a question about what they find confusing.

Power #4: **The Flex Do-Body** power helps you to **use flexible thinking** to choose strategies to use **to do** what's expected.

a. Call on your Social Detective powers and think with your eyes to notice any important clues about a social time. Stop and think about all the smart clues to make a smart guess about what's happening.
b. If you're still unsure about the situation, find someone you trust (like a teacher or parent) who can help you figure it out.
c. If you're in a conversation and hear a joke that you don't understand, laugh along with the others. Later you can ask a close friend or your parents about the joke to find out why it was so funny.
d. If Confusion Carol hangs around when others use words that you don't understand, like informal slang words, fake it at that moment. Your teacher can help you learn more about slang or other tricky words and phrases.

Power #5: **The Cranium Coach** power helps remind you to **use your self-talk** to tell yourself you've done well using new strategies.

- You can tell you've done this today when you can say to yourself:
  "I've figured out social times on my own or with others' help by putting all the clues together."

Stop! The Confuser is invading your brain!

Powers of this Unthinkable

- **The Confuser** gets people to mix up messages they're sending to others with words, their body language, or both. The citizens who are supposed to get the message get confused and maybe even upset when they can't understand.

To do what's expected, use these Superflex strategies:

- Your teachers can help you learn more about the Four Steps of Communication. These steps can help you send the message you want to send and also understand messages that others send you. Here's how it works.

a. Think about the four important parts to communicating a message:
   - Think about the person. Is that person a friend? A stranger? What do you know about the person?
   - Think about the person with your body — your facial expression, body language, and tone of voice.
   - Think about the person with your eyes.
   - Think about the person with your words — what you're asking or what thoughts you're adding.

The Confuser

b. Try to think about putting these together to communicate a clear message. Here is an example:
   - Think: This is a classmate of mine who often talks to me.
   - Body: While I'm sitting in my seat, I'll turn my shoulders to face her, smile, and use a friendly tone of voice.
   - Eyes: I'll think about the person with my eyes to show my interest and to notice clues from the other person.
   - Words: I'll say: "Hey, you got your haircut. It looks good!"

c. As you keep thinking about the other person after you send your message, look for clues that show either interest or confusion. For example, check to see if the person's face looks confused. If that's the case, you may try to find out what she's confused about by saying something friendly like, "You seem confused by my question — did you understand it?" Then try to say it a different way.

Stop! *Thin Flin* is invading your brain!
Use Superflex's Very Cool Five-Step Power Plan to defeat this Unthinkable.

Power #1: **The Decider** power helps you to **stop, describe,** and **decide** the powers of the Unthinkable.

- **Thin Flin** makes people think that they're as thin as a piece of paper and that they won't be noticed if they walk right between people who are having a conversation. But Thin Flin knows this will totally interrupt the conversation!

Power #2: **The Social Detective** power helps you to **observe** the situation and the people in the situation.

- Your Social Detective notices that when people stand in a kind of circle with the front of their shoulders, hips, and feet facing each other it means they're talking or hanging out together. When people are in this kind of group to be together, your detective sees that others walk around that group.

Thin Flin

Power #3: **The Brakester** power helps you to **stop** and **think** to discover the hidden rules.

- It's expected that people observe other citizens who are nearby and especially that they notice who is standing together to talk to each other or to hang out in a group.
- When you see people being part of a group of two or more, it's expected that you'll walk around the group. If you walk through the middle of the group, it makes people think you're being rude to interrupt in this way!

Power #4: **The Flex Do-Body** power helps you to **use flexible thinking** to choose strategies to use **to do** what's expected.

a. Think with your eyes to notice people who are standing in groups and having conversations or hanging out so you'll know to walk around them.
b. To walk around a group, keep your body at least two full arms' length away from them when you're outside in a big open space. Stay about one arm's length away when you're inside and there's not much space because there's a lot of furniture or people. People will notice what you're trying to do so they may move a little to make it easier for you.
c. If you have to walk through a group because there's no space to walk around it, say "Excuse me" as you walk through.

Power #5: **The Cranium Coach** power helps remind you to **use your self-talk** to tell yourself you've done well using new strategies.

- You can tell you've done this today when you can say to yourself:
"I've been noticing when people are standing in groups and I walk around the groups rather than through them!"

Stop! Dark Defeatist is invading your brain!
Use Superflex's Very Cool Five-Step Power Plan to defeat this Unthinkable.

Dark Defeatist

Power #1: **The Decider** power helps you to **stop, describe,** and **decide** the powers of the Unthinkable.

- **Dark Defeatist** comes around when people feel like something is very challenging for them to do. This Unthinkable spreads a self-defeating gloom and doom attitude and makes people give up and feel terrible about themselves.

Power #2: **The Social Detective** power helps you to **observe** the situation and the people in the situation.

- Use your Social Detective powers to observe yourself when you begin to feel that something may take a lot of hard work, like figuring out what to do on a project. Notice if you start to get frustrated and overwhelmed. Your Social Detective sees that often citizens get a bit grumpy when this happens but they try to focus on their inner coach to help them get the task done.

Power #3: **The Brakester** power helps you to **stop** and **think** to discover the hidden rules.

- It's expected that all citizens have difficult things they have to do. They can do their best when they think about how to break down a task into smaller pieces and figure out which parts they know how to do and which parts they may need help with. It's important for citizens to stay calm and stop Dark Defeatist from taking over.

Power #4: **The Flex Do-Body** power helps you to **use flexible thinking** to choose strategies to use **to do** what's expected.

a. Take calming breaths and listen to your inner coach who tells you that you can get through a task that feels difficult if you give yourself enough time and let yourself work on it in smaller parts.
b. Take a movement break!
c. Ask for help from an adult or a fellow student. An adult can also help with breaking down a project into steps or figuring out how you can reward yourself for finishing each step.
d. Remember another time you finished a hard task and how good it felt when you were done!
e. Keep in mind that the time you spend complaining, whining, or even crying is time that you could spend getting help and finishing another step or two of your project.

Power #5: **The Cranium Coach** power helps remind you to **use your self-talk** to tell yourself you've done well using new strategies.

- You can tell you've done this today when you can say to yourself:
"I jump into the cycle of success by saying, 'I can try it.' I move forward and believe in myself, work on a task one step at a time, and ask for help when I need it."

Stop! Armored Alex is invading your brain!

Powers of this Unthinkable

Armored Alex

- Whenever **Armored Alex** senses that something ahead might be hard, he gets people to climb into their shells, shut down, and hide out. This Unthinkable makes people think, "I can't do it" instead of using their superflexible problem-solving skills. When Armored Alex is around, people won't ask for help. It's like they're just in their shells, feeling frustrated and sad.

To do what's expected, use these Superflex strategies:

a. Use self-talk: "I can do this."

b. Think to yourself, "If I haven't tried it, I don't know that I can't do it."

c. Break down the task into three small parts. Take a short break between each part.

d. Remember that even though what you're doing right now may feel hard and boring, it won't last forever. Think about the next fun thing that you'll get to do when you're done.

e. Ask for help from a teacher or friend.

Stop! Disappointed Dan is invading your brain!

Powers of this Unthinkable

Disappointed Dan

- **Disappointed Dan** makes people have disappointed thoughts that are so big that they don't want to do anything else. He gets people to have big reactions like crying and feeling sorry for themselves.

To do what's expected, use these Superflex strategies:

a. Use your inner coach to change those disappointed thoughts to positive, good ones. Remind yourself how positive thoughts make you feel better and send yourself a happier message!

b. Think about what led to being disappointed and stick to the facts. Think about the size of the problem. Maybe the situation feels bigger than it really is, and if you see that it's a small problem, you can have a smaller reaction. Then think of something positive to take your mind off what you were disappointed about.

I CAN'T DO THIS: ARMORED ALEX, DISAPPOINTED DAN
CHAPTER 4 © 2012 SOCIAL THINKING PUBLISHING

c. Keep talking to adults who are helping you with defeating Disappointed Dan. This is a tricky Unthinkable. It may not feel easy to defeat him at first so it's important that you have people around you who can listen to how you feel.

Stop! Kenny Can't is invading your brain!

Powers of this Unthinkable

- **Kenny Can't** makes people say "I can't" when they have work to do. They then give up without trying. When Kenny Can't gets his way, students get frustrated before they even start working and refuse help from teachers.

To do what's expected, use these Superflex strategies:

a. Use self-talk: "I'll try my best."

b. Use calming tools. For example, take deep breaths or count to 10 when you start to notice that Kenny Can't is trying to change your thinking.

c. Use your Social Detective to notice what people around you are thinking and doing. In class, remind yourself that a lot of students are probably defeating Kenny Can't too, because they may not feel like doing work but they know this is part of being a student.

Kenny Can't

d. Think positive thoughts: "I CAN!"

Stop! Negasorus Nix is invading your brain!

Powers of this Unthinkable

- **Negasorus Nix** makes people think negative thoughts and feel they can't do something. This Unthinkable gets people to have thoughts like "I can't" and "It will never work."

To do what's expected, use these Superflex strategies:

a. To defeat Negasorus Nix you have to stay positive. Avoid negative self-talk. If you think you can't do something, tell yourself you can do it. Negative is not the answer. If you don't try, you can never succeed.

b. Ask yourself if you'd rather be positive and successful or negative and frustrated. Look to the guidance of Rainbow Girl, the Thinkable who provides ideas for seeing the bright side of things!

Negasorus Nix

Stop! Refuso is invading your brain!

Powers of this Unthinkable

- **Refuso** gets people to refuse to do things they're asked to do. Refuso make people say things like "I don't think so," "I don't want to!," and "No!"

Refuso

To do what's expected, use these Superflex strategies:

a. Use self-talk: "I can probably do what I want to do later if I do what I'm being asked to do right now."

b. Check what you know about the adult who is asking you to do something. Is this person usually reasonable and fair and someone you trust? If the answer is yes, probably you're being asked to do something that's very reasonable. You need to work on figuring out ways to help yourself get to work!

c. If a parent asks you to do a chore at home, use your self-talk to give yourself a reminder: "I'm a part of the family and everyone is working to do their part. My parents do their chores every day even though some days they may not want to or they're busy with something else. This means I should try to do my part, too."

Stop! *Bored Bobby* is invading your brain!
Use Superflex's Very Cool Five-Step Power Plan to defeat this Unthinkable.

Power #1: The Decider power helps you to **stop, describe,** and **decide** the powers of the Unthinkable.

- **Bored Bobby** gets people to say out loud that they're bored with their teacher, classmates, and other people. He also makes them show that they're bored in other ways — like putting their head down on their desk, pulling out a book to read, looking away, or rolling their eyes when others talk about a topic that doesn't interest them.

Bored Bobby

Power #2: The Social Detective power helps you to **observe** the situation and the people in the situation.

- Your Social Detective notices that others get through a boring moment by staying on task in class or on topic in a conversation (even though they may be thinking they're bored).

Power #3: The Brakester power helps you to **stop** and **think** to discover the hidden rules.

- All people have to do things as part of their day that they may find boring.
- When citizens are in class with you, talking, playing, or hanging out with you, and they feel you're interested in what's going on around you (even if you're not really interested), they feel good about you and how you're behaving.
- Chores and homework you have to do at home can also be boring but your parents are pleased when they can see you've learned to work through tasks you don't like to do.

Power #4: The Flex Do-Body power helps you to **use flexible thinking** to choose strategies to use **to do** what's expected.

a. When you talk with others or are in class dealing with a topic in which you're not interested, fake it and make people feel like you do want to take part. This is called the social fake!
b. When you're doing the social fake, try to:
   - Look at the other person or stay involved in the activity.
   - Use nonverbal cues to show you're interested (like nodding your head or continuing to work on your project).
   - Ask questions about the topic, make a comment, or give short responses ("cool," "hmm," etc.) to show you're listening.

Power #5: The Cranium Coach power helps remind you to **use your self-talk** to tell yourself you've done well using new strategies.

- You can tell you've done this today when you can say to yourself:
"The people around me feel good about talking with me, and the teacher is able to teach her lesson without reminding me to keep my thoughts about being bored in my head."

Stop! *Antsy Nancy* is invading your brain!
Use Superflex's Very Cool Five-Step Power Plan to defeat this Unthinkable.

Power #1: The **Decider** power helps you to **stop, describe,** and **decide** the powers of the Unthinkable.

- **Antsy Nancy** makes people fidget or be impatient.

Power #2: The **Social Detective** power helps you to **observe** the situation and the people in the situation.

- Your Social Detective notices how people's bodies and brains sometimes have a hard time calming down enough to concentrate on their work. To know what strategies will help your body and brain stay focused, your Social Detective has to pay attention to what's happening inside you.

Power #3: The **Brakester** power helps you to **stop** and **think** to discover the hidden rules.

- If people's bodies feel really fidgety or antsy, they need to start by trying to calm down all the activity in their brain. Citizens do this in different ways. Your teacher can share ways to do this.
- People's brains and bodies sometimes feel fidgety or antsy because they're nervous. This can happen when Worry Wall gets involved. You can use Superflex strategies to defeat Worry Wall too!

Antsy Nancy

Power #4: The **Flex Do-Body** power helps you to **use flexible thinking** to choose strategies to use **to do** what's expected.

a. Take calming breaths — take a deep breath and count to 10.
b. Try using an object to fidget with — like a stress ball to squeeze — as long as you and citizens around you can still pay attention. If a fidget distracts you or others, it's a distractor, not a fidget, and may get taken away by teachers or parents.
c. Take a short brain break from your task.
d. Remember that others appreciate it when you work at defeating Antsy Nancy because it helps them stay calm and concentrate too.

Power #5: The **Cranium Coach** power helps remind you to **use your self-talk** to tell yourself you've done well using new strategies.

- You can tell you've done this today when you can say to yourself:
"I've succeeded at getting my body and brain to a calmer place so I can focus on my work or wait for the next thing to happen without feeling like I need to bust out of the room!"

IMPATIENCE: ANTSY NANCY

Stop! Impatient Octopus is invading your brain!

Powers of this Unthinkable

Impatient Octopus

- **Impatient Octopus,** the long-lost cousin of Brain Eater, long ago mastered the art of doing too much at once which, as an octopus, he can do without a problem because, well, he's an octopus with eight tentacles to help him.

- When Impatient Octopus gets in people's brains, he mixes up their thinking so they think they can do a lot of things at once. Because they don't have tentacles, this becomes confusing and frustrating. Impatient Octopus also makes people get impatient easily when things either don't get done or aren't done quickly enough for them and they have to wait.

To do what's expected, use these Superflex strategies:

a. Use your inner coach to remind yourself that you and other citizens of Social Town don't have eight tentacles and that you're only human. This means it may take you time to complete a task or you may even have to wait to take part.

b. If you're waiting for a citizen to do something for you, check for tentacles before you begin to get frustrated. If the citizen doesn't have tentacles, give the person a chance to get things done and allow it to take some time. (P.S. Your answer should always be NO, you and your classmates don't have tentacles! If you notice a human citizen with eight tentacles, you have a problem!)

c. If you notice that something is taking too long, for example, waiting for chicken bites at your local SF Burger Station, and you've done the tentacle check, walk up to someone who can help you. Use friendly words to say that you've been waiting and just wanted to see how long it might take. You can first use your Social Detective powers to observe the situation and make sure there's no reason why something is taking a long time. It could be, for example, that the SF Burger Station is packed with a lot of citizens because it's lunchtime so the kitchen cooks are busy — and they don't have eight tentacles either!

d. When you notice yourself becoming impatient with yourself or others, take some deep breaths to calm your body and then remember what your inner coach might think.

Stop! **Collider** is invading your brain!
Use Superflex's Very Cool Five-Step Power Plan to defeat this Unthinkable.

Power #1: The Decider power helps you to **stop, describe,** and **decide** the powers of the Unthinkable.

- **Collider** makes people interrupt others and create conversational "collisions." Collider gets people to feel like they have to share their information right that minute or they'll forget what they want to say and the conversation will be ruined.

Collider

Power #2: The Social Detective power helps you to **observe** the situation and the people in the situation.

- Your Social Detective notices how others share their ideas pretty quickly with one another in a conversation. As people get older and become stronger social thinkers, they learn to jump in right away with their words as soon as someone finishes their thought. But they avoid interrupting others to share their thoughts.

Power #3: The Brakester power helps you to **stop** and **think** to discover the hidden rules.

- Citizens often have conversations to learn new information and to make others feel that they're interested in them. To keep a conversation going, it's important to let others have a chance to add their information before you jump in with yours while others are talking.

Power #4: The Flex Do-Body power helps you to **use flexible thinking** to choose strategies to use **to do** what's expected.

a. Use self-talk: "It's okay. I can wait my turn to talk or hold my thought and not talk at all. I should focus on what other people are saying rather than just think about what I want to say." "If I forget my thought, it might come back to me in a minute."
b. Think about how interrupting makes others feel frustrated, angry, and annoyed. When you interrupt, others think that you don't care about what they have to say.
c. Practice the back down: If you interrupt and your words collide with someone else's words, stop your words, say something like "you go" (meaning you go first and I'll talk next), let the other person speak, and when that person is done, take your turn to share a small bit of your information.

Power #5: The Cranium Coach power helps remind you to **use your self-talk** to tell yourself you've done well using new strategies.

- You can tell you've done this today when you can say to yourself:
"Other people around me seem like they're enjoying talking to me and look for me to talk with at lunch or recess. Also, my teacher doesn't have to keep telling me to wait to share my ideas."

INTERRUPTING: COLLIDER

CHAPTER 4 © 2012 SOCIAL THINKING PUBLISHING

Stop! Igor Interrupter is invading your brain!

Powers of this Unthinkable

- **Igor Interrupter** gets people to talk when others are talking. This Unthinkable keeps people from waiting for their turn to talk.

To do what's expected, use these Superflex strategies:

a. Use your eyes to notice when other people are talking.

b. When others are speaking, hold your thoughts in your head or write them down to share later.

c. Use your Social Detective powers to see that other people are talking right now or perhaps working quietly and so this isn't a good time to talk.

d. Use self-talk: "I need to wait for my turn or perhaps just write my thought in my thought journal and not even say it out loud!"

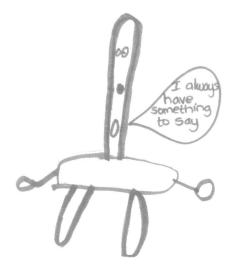

Igor Interrupter

Stop! Int-Erupter is invading your brain!

Powers of this Unthinkable

- **Int-Erupter** gets people to interrupt when others are talking.

To do what's expected, use these Superflex strategies:

a. Use self-talk: "I can keep my thoughts in my thought bubble until it's time to share" or "I can wait my turn to talk."

b. Repeat one of these phrases to yourself as a way to help stay calm and defeat this Unthinkable.

Int-Erupter

Stop! *Inter-Ruptor* is invading your brain!

Inter-Ruptor

Powers of this Unthinkable

- **Inter-Ruptor** gets a person to interrupt others. This might include interrupting a teacher giving directions, blurting out answers, or butting into other people's conversations.

To do what's expected, use these Superflex strategies:

a. Raise your hand and wait to be called on before talking in class.

b. Keep your ideas in your "thinking bubble" until it's your turn to speak out loud or answer a question in class.

c. Wait for a pause in a conversation before taking your turn to speak. Use your Social Detective powers during conversations, meaning you think with your eyes and ears to figure out who is talking to whom and to learn to figure out when someone is about to finish speaking.

d. Be aware that when you interrupt, you may cause others to become mad, sad, or frustrated. If you interrupt too often, others may choose to not talk to you.

e. Remind yourself that you can write your ideas in your thought journal so that you'll remember them later.

f. Before you speak, ask yourself: "How will the teacher, classmates, or friends feel when I say what I'm about to say if I say it right now?"

Superflex also wants you to remember:

- Interrupting during class distracts the teacher and doesn't allow the ideas of your fellow students to be heard by all.

- You can interrupt others not just by talking but by making noises, singing, or yelling when it's time to be listening.

Stop! Interruptagator is invading your brain!

Powers of this Unthinkable

- **Interruptagator** eats other people's words (by snapping with his jaw!) so those people don't have a chance to talk. This can make people feel frustrated and upset and think the person who is interrupting is rude.

To do what's expected, use these Superflex strategies:

- You can think about how a traffic light works to help you defend against Interruptagator.

a. Picture the green, yellow, and red lights on a traffic light.

Interruptagator

b. Think with your eyes as a Social Detective.
   - ◆ Green light: You notice people include you in a discussion and you listen to what people are saying. If you say your own comment after people have come to the end of saying their thoughts, you're at a green light and doing well talking to others. If you're in class, you've raised your hand and are waiting to be called on. People will be pleased that you're taking part in the discussion.
   - ◆ Yellow light: You're thinking with your eyes some of the time but not fully paying attention to who is talking. If a person has completed a thought, you're at risk for making an error. A yellow light is a warning that Interruptagator may get you to try and jump in and interrupt! If you're in class, Interruptagator may not be reminding you to raise your hand, think with your eyes, and expect that you may not get called on even if you have your hand raised. Overpower your Interruptagator by using strategies to defeat him!
   - ◆ Red light: You listen to bits and pieces of what someone else is talking about and you aren't thinking with your eyes or paying attention to what's going on in class. Red light! You're at great risk for interrupting and getting people frustrated with you! Overpower Interruptagator by remembering you're with other people and you have to use your Social Detective to see if it's a good time to share your thoughts. If it's not a good time, keep them in your mind and possibly write them in your thought journal!

Stop! La-Ti-Da is invading your brain!

Powers of this Unthinkable

- **La-Ti-Da** makes people want to sing and hum at times when it's expected they think and listen. When people have a song in their head, La-Ti-Da makes them sing it loud enough for others to hear — even if they're not singing it well! When the volume of the music in their mind is turned up, their Social Detective skills are turned down! This makes it hard for them to focus on what's going on around them and to notice that people may be having weird or uncomfortable thoughts about them!

La-Ti-Da

To do what's expected, use these Superflex strategies:

a. If you're not sure if people can hear your singing, place your index fingers on the bony part of your throat and lightly hold them there for a few seconds. If you can feel your throat vibrating on your fingertips, people can hear you. This is because the vibration means your voice box is making sound. If you can't feel any vibration on your fingers, it likely means your voice is quiet and no one can hear you!

b. If music is playing in your mind, work to keep the volume of your soundtrack turned low by keeping your Social Detective skills turned up HIGH. This lets you pay attention to who is around you and make smart guesses about what they expect from others who are around them. (An expected behavior is likely that you should keep your voice volume and song volume turned down to low or turned off!)

c. Think about what the group is doing and focus on what's expected for you to do.

d. Keep looking for clues about how others are thinking and feeling to figure out if your mind's soundtrack is turned up too high.

e. Make sure you're in an area where no one else is around you before you sing to yourself in a loud voice.

Stop! Concrete Connie is invading your brain!

Use Superflex's Very Cool Five-Step Power Plan to defeat this Unthinkable.

Power #1: **The Decider** power helps you to **stop, describe,** and **decide** the powers of the Unthinkable.

Concrete Connie

- **Concrete Connie** makes people think of only the exact and literal meaning of words. If someone is asked, "What's up?," Concrete Connie gets the person to look up to the sky. Concrete Connie works closely with Rock Brain so that people hear and think about information in only one way.

Power #2: **The Social Detective** power helps you to **observe** the situation and the people in the situation.

- Your Social Detective notices that trying to figure out what someone means by what they say is tricky! Language can be very concrete, which means the meaning doesn't change. A sidewalk is made out of concrete too! In fourth grade, citizens learn that language can also be "figurative," which means you have to "figure it out" to understand the meaning of words. For example, often when people say "What's up?," they really mean "Hi."

Power #3: **The Brakester** power helps you to **stop** and **think** to discover the hidden rules.

- The one big hidden rule is to try and be flexible when trying to figure out what people mean by what they say! Flexible thinking allows for smart guesses.

Power #4: **The Flex Do-Body** power helps you to **use flexible thinking** to choose strategies to use **to do** what's expected.

a. Think with your eyes and ears about the clues that a person gives you to figure out the meaning of what he or she is saying:
   - Who is saying the information to you?
   - Where are you?
   - What's the person saying? Are there two meanings to the words? What does the person's body communicate?
   - What's the person thinking about with her eyes?
   - Smart guess = _____

b. When Concrete Connie has invaded, it's not easy to get help just from Superflex. Your teachers, parents, and speech language pathologist will help you to try to learn more strategies to help you figure this out. It does take a lot of practice!

Power #5: **The Cranium Coach** power helps remind you to **use your self-talk** to tell yourself you've done well using new strategies.

- You can tell you've done this today when you can say to yourself:
  "I've done a good job when I can see I am trying to be flexible in how I interpret what people are saying."

Stop! Empathy Eraser is invading your brain!
Use Superflex's Very Cool Five-Step Power Plan to defeat this Unthinkable.

Power #1: The Decider power helps you to stop, describe, and decide the powers of the Unthinkable.

- **Empathy Eraser** has the power to erase a person's ability to care about other people's feelings. Empathy Eraser then gets the person to do things that hurt other people's feelings without thinking about how this might make them feel.

Power #2: The Social Detective power helps you to observe the situation and the people in the situation.

- Your Social Detective notices that to keep others feeling good people have to consider and understand their thoughts and feelings. This is called having "empathy."

Empathy Eraser

Power #3: The Brakester power helps you to stop and think to discover the hidden rules.

- When citizens are around others, it's expected that they use their Social Detective powers to think about the hidden rules of the situation. It's expected that they check in to see how other people respond to what they say.
- If you aren't sure how someone feels but think you may have said something unexpected or hurtful, it's okay to ask the person about it.

Power #4: The Flex Do-Body power helps you to use flexible thinking to choose strategies to use to do what's expected.

a. Use your inner coach to ask yourself how the words will make the person feel. If the answer is hurtful, mad, or sad, use your brain filter and don't say the words. (A brain filter is a fun way to think about how your brain can help you sort the words that can come out of your mouth so you know which words should stay in your brain.)
b. Use your detective powers to make sure others are giving clues to show they feel comfortable and enjoy talking to you (they're smiling, asking you questions, etc.).

Power #5: The Cranium Coach power helps remind you to use your self-talk to tell yourself you've done well using new strategies.

- You can tell you've done this today when you can say to yourself:
"People around me seem to be enjoying themselves. I may also notice more kids seeking me out to play or hang out because by defeating Empathy Eraser, I make people feel good when they're with me."

Stop! Toxicore is invading your brain!

Powers of this Unthinkable

- **Toxicore** dissolves people's social filters, making them spew out comments that they should keep in their brain. Toxicore's words can seem like toxic waste, causing citizens to get hurt by what's said and ruining friendships.

To do what's expected, use these Superflex strategies:

Toxicore

a. Remember the saying: "If you don't have something nice to say, don't say anything at all!" and use it! If your comments will make someone feel bad, keep them in your mind and don't let them out of your mouth. This is what we call "using a filter"!

b. Another way to look at this is to consider putting a lock box on the social filter in your brain. It's okay to have negative thoughts about people but you need to keep them locked up in your mind. This is especially important to do when you're with the person you feel negative about!

c. Once you've defeated Toxicore, try to repair your friendships! A sincere apology and using your filter and lock box when you're with this person in the future is a great way to clean up a "toxic spill."

d. Everyone makes mistakes with how they treat other people at times. This is why children learn to apologize from a very young age!

e. You can apologize in many different ways. These are some examples of things you can say to a person who you know you hurt:
   - "It wasn't nice of me to say those things. I'm really sorry I hurt your feelings," or
   - "Sorry for being so mean — I was in a really bad mood," or
   - "I'm sorry for what I said. I didn't mean it, I was just upset with things."
   You can use other words too — these are just some ideas for what you can say!

f. Apologizing with words isn't the only way to show you're sorry for what you said or did. Your actions also help. For example, you could let the person you're apologizing to pick what you'll do next or work to show that you're interested in what the person has to say. How you treat citizens through your actions is at least as important as what you say to them.

Stop! *Nosey Rosey* is invading your brain!
Use Superflex's Very Cool Five-Step Power Plan to defeat this Unthinkable.

Power #1: **The Decider** power helps you to **stop, describe,** and **decide** the powers of the Unthinkable.

Nosey Rosey

- **Nosey Rosey** loves to get into people's brains to tempt them to get into other people's business by listening to their conversations and worrying about what everyone else is talking about.

Power #2: **The Social Detective** power helps you to **observe** the situation and the people in the situation.

- Your Social Detective notices that a citizen sometimes overhears other people's conversations and things people say to each other even when that citizen isn't part of the conversation. When this happens, a citizen usually tries to keep herself from actively listening to what's being said.
- If Nosey Rosey gets a person to try to actively listen to what others are saying, it's called eavesdropping or "being nosey." People don't like others to eavesdrop on them.

Power #3: **The Brakester** power helps you to **stop** and **think** to discover the hidden rules.

- If a person isn't part of a conversation, that person should work at avoiding listening to what the others are talking about. If he does hear enough of what the other citizens are saying to have thoughts about it, it's expected that he won't butt in and say what he thinks.

Power #4: **The Flex Do-Body** power helps you to **use flexible thinking** to choose strategies to use **to do** what's expected.

- MYOB — mind your own business. Keep your eyes and ears to yourself. If you're not part of the conversation but can hear what other people are saying, try to:
  a. Walk further away from the people to keep yourself from listening.
  b. Keep yourself from thinking about what you just heard.
  c. Don't tell others what you heard.
  d. Avoid butting into their conversation to tell them what you're thinking or worrying about what you overheard.

Power #5: **The Cranium Coach** power helps remind you to **use your self-talk** to tell yourself you've done well using new strategies.

- You can tell you've done this today when you can say to yourself:
"I'm around others but don't listen to their discussions and don't react to conversations I'm not part of."

NONE OF MY BUSINESS: NOSEY ROSEY

Stop! Perfect Pete is invading your brain!
Use Superflex's Very Cool Five-Step Power Plan to defeat this Unthinkable.

Perfect Pete

Power #1: **The Decider** power helps you to **stop, describe,** and **decide** the powers of the Unthinkable.

- **Perfect Pete** makes people think that everything they do should be perfect. He gets them to think that nothing they ever do is good enough. Perfect Pete may even get people to want to yell at themselves or others when they make a mistake.

Power #2: **The Social Detective** power helps you to **observe** the situation and the people in the situation.

- Even when Perfect Pete is in your brain, your Social Detective notices that parents, teachers, and friends all make little mistakes here and there!

Power #3: **The Brakester** power helps you to **stop** and **think** to discover the hidden rules.

- Everyone is expected to make mistakes throughout the day. Teachers know that students have a lot of work to do and don't expect all work to be perfect or even close to perfect all of the time.

- It's also expected that people can stay calm when they make mistakes. Be aware that Glassman and Worry Wall like to pal around with Perfect Pete and his sister Can't Be Wrong Rita and pal Perfect Patty. They all work as a team to make people stressed, anxious, and upset. They're very powerful!

Power #4: **The Flex Do-Body** power helps you to **use flexible thinking** to choose strategies to use **to do** what's expected.

a. If Perfect Pete is in your brain in a big way, one way to help defeat him is to practice making mistakes. You can play games with your parent or therapist in which you all have fun making little mistakes and see if everyone can laugh about them.
b. Remember that it will be easier to do your work when you know that it doesn't have to be perfect!
c. Use self-talk: "I can allow myself to make at least _____ (fill in a number) mistakes a day."
d. Take deep breaths to stay calm when you notice you've made a mistake or have to turn in work that's less than perfect.

Power #5: **The Cranium Coach** power helps remind you to **use your self-talk** to tell yourself you've done well using new strategies.

- You can tell you've done this today when you can say to yourself:
"I can watch myself make a mistake or turn in a paper that's not perfect and stay calm and happy with my own learning."

Stop! Can't Be Wrong Rita is invading your brain!

Powers of this Unthinkable

- Like Perfect Pete, **Can't Be Wrong Rita** gets people to worry about being wrong and gets them really upset if they make a mistake.

To do what's expected, use these Superflex strategies:

a. When you make a mistake, say "Oops!" or "I forgot!" and smile and laugh or giggle.

b. Use self-talk if you make a mistake. For example: "Other kids won't laugh at me because they make mistakes too! I'm still very smart," "If I'm wrong, people will still like me a lot," and "It's okay to be wrong sometimes because I'm right a lot of times too!"

c. Make your friends feel good — say "Good work!" when they get something right!

d. Watch out for Worry Wall, Glassman, Perfect Pete, and Perfect Patty who also show up with Can't Be Wrong Rita.

e. Also use the Superflex strategy ideas for defeating Perfect Pete.

Can't Be Wrong Rita

Stop! Perfect Patty is invading your brain!

Powers of this Unthinkable

- **Perfect Patty** makes people feel like they always have to be perfect… at EVERYTHING. They have to be perfect at school, homework, writing, drawing, playing games, dancing, and everything else! Perfect Patty makes it hard for people to make mistakes, move on with their work, and stay social because they're so focused on being perfect.

To do what's expected, use these Superflex strategies:

a. Notice that when you have a task to do, you're expected to do the task within a reasonable amount of time. You don't need to do the task perfectly because you don't have hours and hours or days and days to do just one thing. "Do the best you can" is a saying that means you should do the best you can do in the time you have

Perfect Patty

NOT BEING PERFECT: CAN'T BE WRONG RITA, PERFECT PATTY

CHAPTER 4 © 2012 SOCIAL THINKING PUBLISHING

without driving yourself crazy with how perfectly you can do it. For example, when you write a paper, the goal is to practice sharing your ideas in a way that doesn't make you super stressed, eat up all your time, or make you feel bad about yourself or the work.

b. Notice you're naturally good at doing some things more than others. You can't do everything at the same level of perfection!

c. Teachers expect you to learn how to take part in activities and schoolwork and don't expect you to be perfect or even good at everything you try.

d. Learn to use strategies to keep yourself calm, such as closing your eyes, and counting to 10. These can help you move your mind away from whatever is stressing you and let yourself stop pushing to do things perfectly!

Stop! Shurman Shirker is invading your brain!
Use Superflex's Very Cool Five-Step Power Plan to defeat this Unthinkable.

Shurman Shirker

Power #1: **The Decider** power helps you to **stop, describe,** and **decide** the powers of the Unthinkable.

- **Shurman Shirker** convinces people to try and get away with doing the least amount of work possible.
- He encourages them to put off getting started or find a distraction. He often teams up with Dark Defeatist to get people to think that it's not even worth trying.

Power #2: **The Social Detective** power helps you to **observe** the situation and the people in the situation.

- Your Social Detective observes that all citizens have tasks they don't want to do and that students have different strategies they use to get themselves to do their work anyhow. Your Social Detective also notices that negative things can happen if students don't finish or even start their work, like not being able to do a fun activity.

Power #3: **The Brakester** power helps you to **stop** and **think** to discover the hidden rules.

- In school, teachers are there to help students learn how to do the work. This means you have to keep in mind that you can ask your teacher for help with how to get through difficult work. You'll feel better about yourself when you can defeat Shurman Shirker and get your work done. This also helps other citizens feel good about you.

Power #4: **The Flex Do-Body** power helps you to **use flexible thinking** to choose strategies to use **to do** what's expected.

- a. Call on your inner coach to stay positive about your work. "I can do this!"
- b. Take a movement break before starting to work to get your brain ready for thinking.
- c. Break down your task into smaller parts and only work on one part at a time. Your teacher can help with this. Reward yourself with a positive comment after you finish each part.
- d. Set a timer for a certain number of minutes — 7 or 12, for example — and push yourself to keep working for that number of minutes. Then, take a brain and body break and reset the timer.

Power #5: **The Cranium Coach** power helps remind you to **use your self-talk** to tell yourself you've done well using new strategies.

- You can tell you've done this today when you can say to yourself:
  "I'm focusing on being positive about my work and I'm finishing more tasks."

Stop! *Waitin' Mate* is invading your brain!

Powers of this Unthinkable

- **Waitin' Mate** makes you put off doing something you need to do. This is also called "procrastinating."

To do what's expected, use these Superflex strategies:

a. Make a list of what you need to complete and by when. A teacher or parent can help you make the list if you have trouble remembering all the important parts.

b. Create a schedule of your day and block off times to work and times for a break. Then cross things off the schedule as you go.

c. Remember that when you know something needs to be done, it makes you think about it or even worry about it. Once it's done, the worry is done. Doing your work on schedule helps you think and worry about it less!

d. Say to yourself: "It has to get done… do it now so later I can have some fun!"

Waitin' Mate

Stop! *Egg-Certain* is invading your brain!
Use Superflex's Very Cool Five-Step Power Plan to defeat this Unthinkable.

Egg-Certain

Power #1: The Decider power helps you to stop, describe, and decide the powers of the Unthinkable.

- **Egg-Certain** gets people to "crack" by doing unexpected behaviors to try and fit in with their peers. Egg-Certain can also make citizens think that someone is their friend when that "friend" is trying to get them to make bad choices!

Power #2: The Social Detective power helps you to observe the situation and the people in the situation.

- Your Social Detective notices that students aren't always nice to each other. Sometimes students who look like they're acting friendly may be trying to make citizens do unexpected things. Your Social Detective is learning to figure out who are truly nice people and who aren't really friends but are "fake friends."

Power #3: The Brakester power helps you to stop and think to discover the hidden rules.

- Learning who are "real friends" and who are "fake friends" can be tricky. Real friends are nice to you consistently, don't ask you to do things that make you feel uncomfortable, and show they care how you feel. Fake friends may act friendly at certain times or with certain people like teachers. But then they ask you to do something that you know is unexpected or laugh at you after they ask you to do something.

Power #4: The Flex Do-Body power helps you to use flexible thinking to choose strategies to use to do what's expected.

a. Be very aware of your Social Detective to learn to spot real friends and fake friends.
b. Say "No" and walk away if you notice that someone is trying to get you to do something unexpected. You can talk to an adult or someone you trust about ways to say no.
c. If you find people laugh at you after they ask you to do something, there's a good chance they're being very mean. Find a safe adult (a principal or teacher) to talk to about the situation.
d. If you remember that a person has been mean to you in the past but is now acting friendly, be aware that this may be fake friendliness and avoid the trap!

Power #5: The Cranium Coach power helps remind you to use your self-talk to tell yourself you've done well using new strategies.

- You can tell you've done this today when you can say to yourself:
"I can detect the difference between a real friend and a fake friend. I can also notice the good job I'm doing when I say 'No way' to a request a fake friend has made of me."

PEER PRESSURE: EGG-CERTAIN

CHAPTER 4 © 2012 SOCIAL THINKING PUBLISHING

stop! Book Magnet is invading your brain!
Use Superflex's Very Cool Five-Step Power Plan to defeat this Unthinkable.

Power #1: The Decider power helps you to **stop, describe,** and **decide** the powers of the Unthinkable.

- **Book Magnet** pulls people back to books when they're supposed to be working on homework, listening in class, or just playing with friends. Book Magnet makes books so powerful that a person stops thinking about what the group is doing.

Power #2: The Social Detective power helps you to **observe** the situation and the people in the situation.

Book Magnet

- Your Social Detective notices there are times when citizens enjoy doing things by themselves quietly, like reading a book. There are other times when people are expected to spend some time with others. It's important to have a balance between quiet time and social time.

Power #3: The Brakester power helps you to **stop** and **think** to discover the hidden rules.

- There are times that are social experiences, meaning people are expected to talk and relate to those around them, such as during recess and family dinners. Some citizens really like to read books, which have all kinds of cool information. But when others see someone reading, they may think that citizen would rather be with a book than people and isn't interested in them.

Power #4: The Flex Do-Body power helps you to **use flexible thinking** to choose strategies to use **to do** what's expected.

a. Make a schedule for times for reading, studying, and socializing when at school, at home, or when around others during social times.
b. Practice sticking to your schedule during study times. This can mean putting away a book you want to read and reminding yourself you'll feel better about getting your schoolwork done!
c. Practice sticking to your schedule during social times. This usually means you should put the book you want to read in a place where you can't easily see it or get it so it won't distract you.

Power #5: The Cranium Coach power helps remind you to **use your self-talk** to tell yourself you've done well using new strategies.

- You can tell you've done this today when you can say to yourself:
"I'm able to get my homework and classwork done, have some people to hang out with or play with at school, and find time to read my book. When this happens, my life is more in balance."

Power #1: **The Decider** power helps you to **stop, describe,** and **decide** the powers of the Unthinkable.

Hermit Crab

- **Hermit Crab** makes people want to stay inside playing video games and watching TV rather than going outside to play or be social with friends. This Unthinkable may also get citizens to think that it's just easier to stay inside by themselves than to go out and try to be social.

Power #2: **The Social Detective** power helps you to **observe** the situation and the people in the situation.

- Your Social Detective observes that citizens of all ages enjoy hanging out with others, which is shown by their friendly body language and words with one another. Everyone is different in how comfortable they feel hanging out with others. Some people even get nervous at the thought of going out and spending time with people.

Power #3: **The Brakester** power helps you to **stop** and **think** to discover the hidden rules.

- It's expected that people make attempts to socialize and do activities that let them be around other people. Sometimes these social moments involve a particular interest, like chess club or a sport. It's also expected that people try to create a schedule for themselves when they're not in school that includes a lot of different activities (alone and with others).
- If people don't leave their houses much to socialize, it's natural for citizens to wonder why. They might even think the citizen is trying to stay away from them or is unfriendly.

Power #4: **The Flex Do-Body** power helps you to **use flexible thinking** to choose strategies to use **to do** what's expected.

a. Make a schedule for the times you're not in school with a good balance of times for homework, social time, and alone time. An adult can help with this.
b. Use your inner coach: "I really want to finish this level on my video game, but I said I'd go see my friends now. I'll get to play my video game another time. This is a tiny problem."
c. Keep working with your teacher to learn ways to connect and hang out with others. Being social isn't easy and it's helpful to get support.
d. Work with your parents to come up with activities outside the house that you could go to.

Power #5: **The Cranium Coach** power helps remind you to **use your self-talk** to tell yourself you've done well using new strategies.

- You can tell you've done this today when you can say to yourself:
"I've noticed myself getting out of the house more for social things. I also see that others are wanting to hang out with me outside of school."

Stop! *Sticky Fingers* is invading your brain!
Use Superflex's Very Cool Five-Step Power Plan to defeat this Unthinkable.

Power #1: **The Decider** power helps you to **stop, describe,** and **decide** the powers of the Unthinkable.

- When **Sticky Fingers** gets in people's brains, they get greedy and think that it's okay for them to take whatever they want. Sticky Fingers makes normally law-abiding citizens keep things they find, take things without asking, and even steal things outright!

Power #2: **The Social Detective** power helps you to **observe** the situation and the people in the situation.

- Your Social Detective is on the prowl for citizens who treat each other well. Part of doing this is not taking things from a person without that person's permission.

Sticky Fingers

Power #3: **The Brakester** power helps you to **stop** and **think** to discover the hidden rules.

- Don't steal things from people! Also, if you borrow an object, it's expected you had permission from the owner.

Power #4: **The Flex Do-Body** power helps you to **use flexible thinking** to choose strategies to use **to do** what's expected.

a. Be thankful for what you have.
b. Ask before borrowing something; if you don't do this, you're stealing!
c. Think about how badly you would probably feel if a person took an object from you without asking.
d. Turn in things you find that don't belong to you.
e. Stop and think about what will happen if you steal something. You'll receive a punishment from an adult and other kids may treat you badly because you treated one of them badly by stealing. This will likely make you feel bad or mad.
f. If you're tempted to take something that doesn't belong to you, take a deep breath and walk away from the thing that's tempting you.

Power #5: **The Cranium Coach** power helps remind you to **use your self-talk** to tell yourself you've done well using new strategies.

- You can tell you've done this today when you can say to yourself:
"I haven't taken items that don't belong to me and I'm learning to admire more objects instead of always asking to borrow them."

Stop! Garbage Can Crew *is invading your brain!*
Use Superflex's Very Cool Five-Step Power Plan to defeat this Unthinkable.

Power #1: **The Decider** power helps you to **stop, describe,** and **decide** the powers of the Unthinkable.

Garbage Can Crew

- **Garbage Can Crew** makes people want to talk trash, like use curse words, say gross things, or say mean things about other people.

Power #2: **The Social Detective** power helps you to **observe** the situation and the people in the situation.

- Your Social Detective notices that citizens are usually pretty nice to each other. Your detective observes that there are places and times when citizens avoid using bad words and curse words.
- Sometimes kids joke around with their friends by using curse words, saying gross things, and maybe even talking badly about other people. Using your detective powers, you see that they only do this some of the time and around some people.

Power #3: **The Brakester** power helps you to **stop** and **think** to discover the hidden rules.

- When you're not sure how people will react to the words you say or they've told you before not to say them, don't use curse words or any words that people could think are mean! It's also expected that you won't use swear words or say gross things with people who you know really don't like them.

- Being careful about what to say and when to say it is part of what is called "having good manners." If you say things and do things that make people feel comfortable around you, they're more likely to want to be with you.

Power #4: **The Flex Do-Body** power helps you to **use flexible thinking** to choose strategies to use **to do** what's expected.

a. Remember your manners! Think about where you are and what behavior is expected at that time.
b. Listen to the thoughts in your head and block yourself from saying words other people may find annoying or just plain rude!
c. Use the Grandma Rule. If you wouldn't say it in front of your grandmother, it's best to keep your thoughts in your head and not say them.

Power #5: **The Cranium Coach** power helps remind you to **use your self-talk** to tell yourself you've done well using new strategies.

- You can tell you've done this today when you can say to yourself:
  "I've kept myself from using words that make people have weird thoughts about me."

Stop! Potty Mouth Pete is invading your brain!

Powers of this Unthinkable

- **Potty Mouth Pete** makes people say bad words.

To do what's expected, use these Superflex strategies:

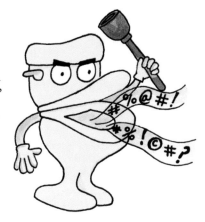

Potty Mouth Pete

a. Close your mouth and keep your words in your head. Tell yourself, "These words are unexpected and make other citizens feel uncomfortable in a way that makes them not want to be with me."

b. Come up with better, expected words to let people know how you feel, what you think, and what you want.

c. Talk to an adult who you trust about why Potty Mouth Pete keeps showing up in your brain. Tell the adult how you really want people to think about you — good and comfortable thoughts or weird and uncomfortable thoughts.

d. Think about the fact that everyone has thoughts about us. These thoughts are either blue thoughts (good thoughts) or red thoughts (not-so-good thoughts). Think about your red thoughts and blue thoughts behaviors and how you have a choice about how people think about some of what you do.

e. Use a journal to write down your thoughts and feelings when you're feeling uncomfortable and Potty Mouth Pete keeps trying to defeat your Superflex thinking.

f. Identify a positive role model in your Social Town. Learn what you can do and say that helps them have more comfortable or good thoughts about you (blue thoughts).

Stop! **Ruler Rod** is invading your brain!
Use Superflex's Very Cool Five-Step Power Plan to defeat this Unthinkable.

Power #1: **The Decider** power helps you to **stop, describe,** and **decide** the powers of the Unthinkable.

- **Ruler Rod** makes a person correct other people and think about rules all the time. When Ruler Rod is at work, the person tells others what they're doing wrong or what rules they're breaking.

Power #2: **The Social Detective** power helps you to **observe** the situation and the people in the situation.

- Your Social Detective notices that everyone makes mistakes at times.

Power #3: **The Brakester** power helps you to **stop** and **think** to discover the hidden rules.

Ruler Rod

- When a mistake is made, there are some times when it's expected that a citizen lets others know about the mistake. There are other times when a mistake should be filed away in a part of a person's brain that can be called a "lock box." Your lock box has a lot of information in it that you noticed but decided not to report.
- It's expected that the people who point out other citizens' mistakes are the ones whose job it is to teach citizens new skills, like teachers, parents, tutors, and therapists.

Power #4: **The Flex Do-Body** power helps you to **use flexible thinking** to choose strategies to use **to do** what's expected.

a. To decide whether to report a mistake, stop and think about how big a problem the mistake could cause. If it means someone could be in physical danger, like if something is going to fall on someone, you should report it right away. If the mistake results in a small problem and it's not your job to correct that person, ignore the mistake and keep it in your lock box.
b. Think about how embarrassed people would feel if their mistake is reported. Embarrassment is a feeling people may have when they worry others are having uncomfortable thoughts about them.
c. Stop and think: "Is it my job to correct this person?," "Is it a big problem or a small one?," and "Will the embarrassment caused by reporting a mistake lead to a bigger problem than the mistake itself?"

Power #5: **The Cranium Coach** power helps remind you to **use your self-talk** to tell yourself you've done well using new strategies.

- You can tell you've done this today when you can say to yourself:
"I've been able to store many thoughts in my lock box and notice that people don't think I'm trying to embarrass them."

Stop! *Tattle Taylor* is invading your brain!

Powers of this Unthinkable

- **Tattle Taylor** makes people tattle, complain, or report the mistakes of others.

To do what's expected, use these Superflex strategies:

a. Write down your problem or worry on a piece of paper. Put it in your tattle box for your teacher to read at a different time. (A teacher can have a tattle box for some students or for the whole class to help people change their tattling behaviors.) Once the paper goes into the box, let the teacher take over and handle the situation.

b. Ask yourself: "Is this a big problem or a small problem and is it my problem?" Use strategies you have already to work through big and small problems. If a problem doesn't belong to you, you should work to let it go and know that the other students will have to deal with their problem. Sometimes, trying to handle a problem that isn't yours can create a problem for you because you're getting involved.

c. Ask yourself: "Is this problem or worry hurting me or someone else?" If the answer is yes, tell an adult right away. If the answer is no, let the teacher worry about everyone else, and you worry about you.

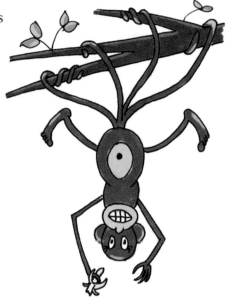

Tattle Taylor

Stop! *Falsificator* is invading your brain!
Use Superflex's Very Cool Five-Step Power Plan to defeat this Unthinkable.

Power #1: The Decider power helps you to **stop, describe,** and **decide** the powers of the Unthinkable.

- **Falsificator** gets people to say things that are false instead of the truth. Falsificator often teams up with Attention Eater to make a person say something untrue as a way of getting attention.

Falsificator

Power #2: The Social Detective power helps you to **observe** the situation and the people in the situation.

- A special task for your Social Detective is to remember how you feel about people when you know they're telling you lies or you find out that they lied to you.
- Notice that you probably find it frustrating when someone lies to you and you may begin to stop trusting that person. Your detective observes how citizens trust people who tell them the truth about most things. They tend to avoid being with people they can't trust because of their lies.

Power #3: The Brakester power helps you to **stop** and **think** to discover the hidden rules.

- It's expected that you tell people the truth about what you know or what you've done.

Power #4: The Flex Do-Body power helps you to **use flexible thinking** to choose strategies to use **to do** what's expected.

a. STOP yourself before you speak by putting your finger to your mouth (to quiet anything that isn't true). Then use self-talk: "Is what I'm about to say the truth?"
b. Remind yourself how you want people to include you and that one big way for this to happen is for others to trust you.
c. Think about the fact that others will find out the truth later. Lying will only make the problem bigger in the future and make you stand out with your classmates if you begin to lie a lot.

Power #5: The Cranium Coach power helps remind you to **use your self-talk** to tell yourself you've done well using new strategies.

- You can tell you've done this today when you can say to yourself:
"I've done a good job when I've blocked my plan to tell a lie. I'm proud of myself for being honest and for telling people things about myself and others that they'll find are true."

TELLING LIES: FALSIFICATOR
CHAPTER 4 © 2012 SOCIAL THINKING PUBLISHING

Stop! Captain Blame-O is invading your brain!

Powers of this Unthinkable

- **Captain Blame-O** gets people to blame others for things they've done wrong. Sometimes, Worry Wall teams up with Captain Blame-O to make a person worry so much about a problem or a mistake that the person lies to try to keep from getting in trouble.

To do what's expected, use these Superflex strategies:

a. Stop and think about the fact that people may not trust you or feel very good about you if you lie and blame someone else so that you can stay out of trouble.

b. Use self-talk: "Everyone makes mistakes. I have a team of citizens around to help me solve problems, so I should just be honest and tell them I was the one who made a mistake."

Captain Blame-O

c. Think about how honesty makes people feel comfortable and builds trust. If you admit that you're in the wrong even when it's hard, others will be more likely to believe you in the future.

Stop! Storyteller is invading your brain!

Powers of this Unthinkable

- **Storyteller** gets people to tell lies, usually to keep from getting in trouble or to try to get someone else in trouble. This Unthinkable may also show up during school or homework times to get citizens to tell lies to avoid doing their work.

To do what's expected, use these Superflex strategies:

a. Remind yourself that telling lies almost always ends up with the liar getting in even more trouble.

Storyteller

b. Stop and remember that people often know the truth and that you want others to think you're honest. Telling the truth to other citizens will help them trust you and be interested in what you have to say.

c. Classmates at school are often pretty good at detecting lies. Getting caught in a lie can make you stand out more than you thought it would make you fit in. It's not usually worth the risk!

d. Use your imaginary "lie filter" in your brain and if you notice you are about to tell a lie, keep it in your brain.

Stop! T.S. (Thumb Sucker) is invading your brain!
Use Superflex's Very Cool Five-Step Power Plan to defeat this Unthinkable.

Power #1: **The Decider** power helps you to **stop, describe, and decide** the powers of the Unthinkable.

- **T.S.** makes people think that they need to put their thumb in their mouth. Thumb Sucker can take over when people are sleepy, bored, or just aren't paying attention to who is around them and what those people might be thinking.

Power #2: **The Social Detective** power helps you to **observe** the situation and the people in the situation.

- Your Social Detective notices that all students get bored sometimes at school and many feel sleepy. But they usually keep their thumb out of their mouth even during these times.

T.S. (Thumb Sucker)

Power #3: **The Brakester** power helps you to **stop** and **think** to discover the hidden rules.

- A lot of social rules are different for different ages of citizens. It's expected for babies and even toddlers to suck their thumb, but it's not expected for school age students to put their thumb in their mouth as a way to be calm.
- Some citizens do have more of a need to suck on things when they feel upset or stressed. It's a better choice to suck on something that's more expected for the person's age group.

Power #4: **The Flex Do-Body** power helps you to **use flexible thinking** to choose strategies to use **to do** what's expected.

- a. Find ways to stay calm when you're bored or tired at school other than sucking your thumb. You can ask the occupational therapist at your school for some ideas.
- b. Remember that you want the other students to think you're able to stay calm and be focused much like them. You can use a different way to stay calm.
- c. Tell yourself: "When I feel my thumb slipping into my mouth, I'll pull it out and remember a different way to get calm that's more like something someone my age would do. The new behavior I'll start to do when I feel my thumb creeping up toward my mouth is this:

_____."

Power #5: **The Cranium Coach** power helps remind you to **use your self-talk** to tell yourself you've done well using new strategies.

- You can tell you've done this today when you can say to yourself:
"I've been able to keep my thumb out of my mouth during the day and instead use my new strategy!"

THUMB SUCKING: T.S. (THUMB SUCKER)

CHAPTER 4 © 2012 SOCIAL THINKING PUBLISHING

Stop! *Big Bubble Bob* and *Space Squid*
are invading your brain!

Use Superflex's Very Cool Five-Step Power Plan to defeat these Unthinkables.

Power #1: **The Decider** power helps you to **stop, describe,** and **decide** the powers of the Unthinkable.

- **Big Bubble Bob** gets people to leave too much space between them and others. **Space Squid** makes them squeeze too close to other people.

Power #2: **The Social Detective** power helps you to **observe** the situation and the people in the situation.

- Your Social Detective sees that how far people stand apart from each other is based on the situation and who the people are. When citizens aren't having a conversation or planning to have one, your Social Detective notices they often stand away from each other by about two arms' length. They stand closer — about one arm's length — if they're talking or planning to talk with each other.

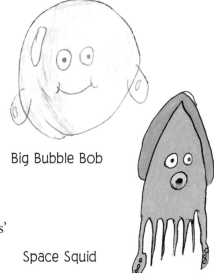

Big Bubble Bob

Space Squid

Power #3: **The Brakester** power helps you to **stop** and **think** to discover the hidden rules.

- The hidden rule: People work at figuring out how far away or how close they should be to other people based on if they want to talk with them or not.
- When Space Squid makes you stand too close to people, this can make them feel uncomfortable, nervous, or even mad because they think you're not thinking of them. If Big Bubble Bob has too much power in your brain, you may be so far away from people that they don't know that you want to talk and hang out with them.

Power #4: **The Flex Do-Body** power helps you to **use flexible thinking** to choose strategies to use **to do** what's expected.

a. Stand about one arm's length away from the people you're talking to. Also have your head, toes, hips, and shoulders pointed toward those people. Stand about two arms' length away from people you're near but not talking with or don't plan to talk with.

b. Get help from the Thinkable Space Respecter who can help you keep both Big Bubble Bob and Space Squid from appearing!

Power #5: **The Cranium Coach** power helps remind you to **use your self-talk** to tell yourself you've done well using new strategies.

- You can tell you've done this today when you can say to yourself:
"People know I'm standing near them when I want to talk with them and they know when I'm not planning to speak. They also don't seem to be annoyed with me for standing too close!"

Stop! *Volume Volumizer* is invading your brain!

Use Superflex's Very Cool Five-Step Power Plan to defeat this Unthinkable.

Power #1: **The Decider** power helps you to stop, describe, and decide the powers of the Unthinkable.

- **Volume Volumizer** takes away people's power to figure out how loudly they should talk at different times. This Unthinkable gets people to think the louder they talk, the more others will listen.

Power #2: **The Social Detective** power helps you to observe the situation and the people in the situation.

- To detect how loudly people need to talk in a situation, your Social Detective observes what people are doing, how many people are in a place, and how far apart they are from each other. When a lot of people are in one place or are spread out across a large outdoor space or room, your Social Detective notices that people often use a louder voice to try to be heard than at other times.

Volume Volumizer

Power #3: **The Brakester** power helps you to stop and think to discover the hidden rules.

- It's expected that citizens change their voice volume based on the type of event and the number of people they're talking to. If you speak so loudly that others stop and turn to look at you, this can make others have weird thoughts. They may think you're trying to get a lot of extra people's attention by using a loud voice. This can also make it hard for them to focus on what they're doing.

Power #4: **The Flex Do-Body** power helps you to use flexible thinking to choose strategies to use to do what's expected.

- a. Use your Social Detective to try and figure out how loud a voice is expected in a specific situation and group.
- b. Listen to how loud your voice is compared to other people and change your vocal volume to match how others sound.
- c. If you find it hard to know how loud or quiet your voice sounds when you talk, you can ask a parent or teacher for help with ways to practice this. For example, you could do this with a volume meter from an electronics store or with some computer games or apps.

Power #5: **The Cranium Coach** power helps remind you to use your self-talk to tell yourself you've done well using new strategies.

- You can tell you've done this today when you can say to yourself:
  "I've changed my vocal volume so I sound like other people I'm around. I know it takes practice to do this for different places and groups."

TOO LOUD: VOLUME VOLUMIZER

Stop! **Information Station** is invading your brain!
Use Superflex's Very Cool Five-Step Power Plan to defeat this Unthinkable.

Power #1: **The Decider** power helps you to **stop, describe,** and **decide** the powers of the Unthinkable.

- **Information Station** makes people share so much of what they know about something that there's not enough time for other people to share their own ideas. When this Unthinkable is around, people think they should share their information at any time, at any place, and with any person.

Power #2: **The Social Detective** power helps you to **observe** the situation and the people in the situation.

- Your Social Detective observes what kind of talking is happening, a conversation for fun, a meeting, or a class discussion. Your detective notices how other students are behaving when they're supposed to be listening to you speak. Do they look like they're interested, distracted, or bored?

Information Station

Power #3: **The Brakester** power helps you to **stop** and **think** to discover the hidden rules.

- Citizens are interested in what other people know but not too much. It's expected that people will share information without taking too much time to speak (ten seconds or less) or by only saying one to two sentences at one time. If one citizen talks a whole lot about a topic, this means that other citizens won't have time to share what they know or talk about things that interest them.

Power #4: **The Flex Do-Body** power helps you to **use flexible thinking** to choose strategies to use to do what's expected.

a. When you speak, stay aware of who you're talking to and why you're talking to that person or group. If you're having a friendly conversation, tell people one or two sentences about the topic. If you're sharing information in class, only share the part the teacher asked about.
b. Observe how much of the time you're talking and make sure to give other people turns to talk.
c. Notice how people are listening to you. If they don't seem interested, stop talking about what you know and ask a question about them.

Power #5: **The Cranium Coach** power helps remind you to **use your self-talk** to tell yourself you've done well using new strategies.

- You can tell you've done this today when you can say to yourself:
  "I'm in control of Information Station when I see other people are sharing information with me. Also, others are telling me more about what they think and feel."

Stop! Dr. Downloader is invading your brain!

Powers of this Unthinkable

- **Dr. Downloader** makes people talk on and on about things they like to think about and to give too many details. This doctor gets citizens to think more about the topic than the people they're with.

To do what's expected, use these Superflex strategies:

a. Learn about what topics are in your own people file (your interests). Dr. Downloader will try to get you to "plug in" to your own file and download and talk about all the things in your people file. But if you know what topics are in your file, you can stop Dr. Downloader before you start to talk about those things. Switch over to your friends' people files and try to ask them questions about their interests. For example, if you're downloading about a history topic, ask others about their favorite type of history or what they're learning about history in their class. Then try to add thoughts to their ideas to keep the conversation going.

b. Practice giving two or three short bits of information about the story, movie, or other topic you're talking about. It's expected to give just a little information at a time so others can jump in with what they want to say.

c. When you're talking, remember to use the clues they give you to see if others are still interested. Are they looking and thinking about you? Are they nodding their heads up and down? Are they adding their words to the topic or are you doing most of the talking? Are people trying to change the topic?

d. If you realize that they're losing interest or that you're taking over the talking time, quickly switch your thoughts to think about the other people you're with. Try listening more to what people are sharing instead of feeling like you have to add a lot to the conversation.

e. When you catch Dr. Downloader at work getting you to take up a lot of the talking time, ask other students questions about their interests or try to make the topic about them.

Dr. Downloader

TOO MUCH INFORMATION: DR. DOWNLOADER

CHAPTER 4 © 2012 SOCIAL THINKING PUBLISHING

Stop! Talks Too Much Tess is invading your brain!

• **Talks Too Much Tess** makes people talk about everything they're thinking about, all the time.

Talks Too Much Tess

To do what's expected, use these Superflex strategies:

a. Stop and look to see if others are looking at you or paying attention to you. Stop talking if they aren't listening.

b. Ask yourself: "Am I giving other people a chance to talk?" If not, stop yourself from talking and try to ask a question so someone else can take a turn talking.

c. Tell yourself: "I don't have to say everything I'm thinking."

d. Work on "active listening" rather than active talking. Active listening is really thinking about what the person is saying and showing interest with your body (your head nods, your shoulders face the person). People really notice when others are good listeners.

e. Write down your thoughts in a journal. You may want to remember them yourself, even if other people don't have time to hear all of them. You can create a special name for your journal and keep it near you in class or at home so you can write in it.

Stop! *Negative Nick* is invading your brain!
Use Superflex's Very Cool Five-Step Power Plan to defeat this Unthinkable.

Power #1: The Decider power helps you to **stop, describe,** and **decide** the powers of the Unthinkable.

I had a boring day! — I didn't have any fun! How was your day? — Bad!

Negative Nick

- **Negative Nick** makes people focus on the negative, or bad, parts of life and gets them to say only negative things.

Power #2: The Social Detective power helps you to **observe** the situation and the people in the situation.

- At most times, your Social Detective observes that there's something positive or good you can notice and also something negative or bad. What you focus on often affects how you feel about what's happening around you.

- One example is if you notice that what your group is talking about at lunch is pretty boring. You then focus on it being boring. This makes you think, "I hate being with these students because they're boring." It may even make you say, "You guys are so boring!" If you say this, you may notice that others decide they'd rather not be with you! Now you're not only bored but lonely too.

Power #3: The Brakester power helps you to **stop** and **think** to discover the hidden rules.

- Citizens don't like to be with people who are always negative. If one person is super negative all the time, it rubs off on others and gives them uncomfortable thoughts about the person. This means you need to try to notice good things and not just bad ones.

- If people tell you to stop being so negative all the time, Negative Nick is getting too much power in your brain!

Power #4: The Flex Do-Body power helps you to **use flexible thinking** to choose strategies to use **to do** what's expected.

a. Stop and think: "How will others feel if I make this negative comment? How can I change it to a positive comment?"
b. Use self-talk: "It wasn't all bad," "There were some things I liked," "I'll try," and "People have good thoughts about me when I try to say friendly words."
c. If a negative comment you want to make will make others feel frustrated, put it in a lock box in your mind and don't say it to the group.

Power #5: The Cranium Coach power helps remind you to **use your self-talk** to tell yourself you've done well using new strategies.

- You can tell you've done this today when you can say to yourself:
"I'm glad people notice I have been making more positive comments; people seem to include me more and aren't telling me to stop being so negative!"

TOO NEGATIVE: NEGATIVE NIX

CHAPTER 4 © 2012 SOCIAL THINKING PUBLISHING

Stop! The Bad Exampler is invading your brain!

Powers of this Unthinkable

- **The Bad Exampler** gets people to act in unexpected ways. This Unthinkable can make people do things like sing songs with bad language or dress in ways not okay for school.

To do what's expected, use these Superflex strategies:

a. Talk to an adult who you trust about why this Unthinkable keeps showing up in your brain. Tell the adult how you'd really like people to think about you. Do you want them to have good thoughts or weird and uncomfortable thoughts about you?

b. Think about red stick (negative) and blue stick (positive) behaviors and how you have a choice with how people think about some of the things you do.

c. Use a journal to write down your thoughts and feelings when you feel uncomfortable or stressed.

d. Use your Social Detective to locate a person who keeps The Bad Exampler under control. Notice how that person behaves when they are having fun and also observe how people respond to that person. Try to copy some of the positive things this person does and see if people respond to you as if you're setting a good example! P.S. When you find a person to observe to figure out how to behave in a more blue stick (positive) way, this person is called a "role model."

The Bad Exampler

Stop! Dream Catcher is invading your brain!
Use Superflex's Very Cool Five-Step Power Plan to defeat this Unthinkable.

Power #1: The Decider power helps you to **stop, describe,** and **decide** the powers of the Unthinkable.

- **Dream Catcher** makes people think a few hours of sleep a night is plenty to get them through the school day. Dream Catcher gets people to feel so tired — or think they're so tired — that they even close their eyes to sleep at unexpected times.

Power #2: The Social Detective power helps you to **observe** the situation and the people in the situation.

- Your Social Detective notices that other citizens may come to school talking about how they're tired. But when the class starts or they're in a conversation, they try to not show that they're sleepy.

Dream Catcher

Power #3: The Brakester power helps you to **stop** and **think** to discover the hidden rules.

- When a teacher is teaching a lesson or a classmate is talking, it's expected that students look at and think about the speaker with their eyes so the speaker feels like they're listening. Citizens know that people have many bored or tired moments during a day, but it's expected they'll do the "social fake" and get through them.

Power #4: The Flex Do-Body power helps you to **use flexible thinking** to choose strategies to use **to do** what's expected.

a. Plan when you need to go to sleep to get about eight hours of rest. Create a sleep routine so that you always do the same things, like brushing your teeth or reading a book, to get your brain ready for sleep.

b. Try to keep your body healthy by getting enough sleep, exercising, and eating healthy foods because this helps to keep it feeling good and keeps your brain awake!

c. To get through a tired moment at school, sit up and keep your head up. Look toward the person who's talking and give clues with your body that you're paying attention, like nodding your head to agree. Add your ideas to the topic and keep any "I'm tired" thoughts in your brain.

d. If you've worked hard to keep your body healthy and still feel tired all the time, talk to one of your parents. You may need to go to the doctor!

Power #5: The Cranium Coach power helps remind you to **use your self-talk** to tell yourself you've done well using new strategies.

- You can tell you've done this today when you can say to yourself:
"I'm able to stay connected longer in class, look interested and alert when I talk with friends, and my overall energy feels better throughout my day."

TOO TIRED: DREAM CATCHER

Stop! *Bedman* is invading your brain!

Powers of this Unthinkable

- **Bedman** gets people to sleep during class time and to not feel like doing any work because of being too tired.

To do what's expected, use these Superflex strategies:

a. Ask your teacher if you can go get a drink of water or go to the sink to wash your face.

b. Ask your teacher if you can stand up at your desk and stretch to wake up your body.

c. Wiggle your toes under your desk but make sure not to distract anyone else.

d. Use a scale to map out your levels of being tired so you can try to catch yourself early and defeat Bedman before it gets harder.

Bedman

stop! Professorus Wrecks is invading your brain!
Use Superflex's Very Cool Five-Step Power Plan to defeat this Unthinkable.

Power #1: The Decider power helps you to **stop, describe,** and **decide** the powers of the Unthinkable.

Professorus Wrecks

- **Professorus Wrecks** is a master at getting people to use too many adult words or formal language at unexpected times. This Unthinkable also makes people use words that others don't understand.

Power #2: The Social Detective power helps you to **observe** the situation and the people in the situation.

- Your Social Detective sees that citizens change what words they use and how they talk based on the people they're talking with. For example, as children get older, they start using more informal words to speak to one another. They may even use "slang" words like "What's up" instead of "Hi" to greet someone their own age.
- Your detective also observes that citizens try not to use words that are hardly ever used or words that are hard for people to understand.

Power #3: The Brakester power helps you to **stop** and **think** to discover the hidden rules.

- It's expected that citizens think about the people they're with and how they might have to change the words they use for different groups of people. It's also expected that students use words that match their age.

Power #4: The Flex Do-Body power helps you to **use flexible thinking** to choose strategies to use **to do** what's expected.

a. You may find it easier to keep adult words in your brain locker unless you're speaking to adults. Even then, don't use them too much.
b. Use self-talk to figure out if the words are expected by asking yourself: "Have I heard this group of people use these words?" and "Based on what I know about these people, will they know and understand these words?"
c. If you notice a lot of students using slang at school, you can talk to a parent, teacher, or therapist about learning more of these words.

Power #5: The Cranium Coach power helps remind you to **use your self-talk** to tell yourself you've done well using new strategies.

- You can tell you've done this today when you can say to yourself:
"I've talked with others and they appear to be enjoying themselves or appear interested during the conversation. I'm also thinking more about the words that I use and trying to make small word changes when I'm with others."

WORDS YOU USE: PROFESSORUS WRECKS
CHAPTER 4 © 2012 SOCIAL THINKING PUBLISHING

Stop! **Negative Future Charge** is invading your brain!
Use Superflex's Very Cool Five-Step Power Plan to defeat this Unthinkable.

Power #1: **The Decider** power helps you to **stop, describe,** and **decide** the powers of the Unthinkable.

- **Negative Future Charge** forces people to focus on the future, worrying only about negative outcomes of future events.

Power #2: **The Social Detective** power helps you to **observe** the situation and the people in the situation.

- Your Social Detective notices that people grow up and learn more skills with each week, month, and year of life. You can use your detective powers to see how different high school students and adults are from elementary school age children. Look in a mirror and see that you're still learning as well!

Negative Future Charge

Power #3: **The Brakester** power helps you to **stop** and **think** to discover the hidden rules.

- Citizens keep learning throughout their lives. Even adults don't know what job they'll get or all the things they'll do in their lives!

Power #4: **The Flex Do-Body** power helps you to **use flexible thinking** to choose strategies to use **to do** what's expected.

a. If you worry about what you'll become when you get older, here are things to focus on:
- Notice that you're learning so much all the time that you can't imagine how much you'll know by the time you're an adult. Your focus now should be on continuing to learn information and how to be with other people, which includes making and keeping new friends.
- Help yourself to see how much you've been learning by noticing what you learned in the grades before the one you're in now. Notice what you've been learning every week this year. Now think about how much more you'll learn as you continue to grow up.
- Continue to learn about being flexible and how being flexible will help you when you grow up. Children are expected to think of all the different things they may want to do in their lives and to keep learning a whole bunch of different information. When you get older, you can use some of this information in one job and use other information in another job.
b. If Negative Future Charge tries to take over the powers in your brain, remind yourself to focus on what you're doing today and learning this week so you'll have more skills for when you get older.

Power #5: **The Cranium Coach** power helps remind you to **use your self-talk** to tell yourself you've done well using new strategies.

- You can tell you've done this today when you can say to yourself:
"I'm able to focus on what I'm doing right now. I avoid worrying about what my life will be like when I become an adult."

Stop! Mr. Whoemeye is invading your brain!

Powers of this Unthinkable

- **Mr. Whoemeye** makes people worry about their future and who and what they'll become. This worry gets people to try to act like different people or characters they may want to be like when they grow up, like a rap singer or a superhero. When they do this, other students may get confused about why they're acting this way. Mr. Whoemeye likes to get everyone confused!

To do what's expected, use these Superflex strategies:

a. Citizens think it can be fun when people use their imagination and pretend to be different people or characters during certain play times. Work at learning when those imaginary or pretend times might be at school. Students older than kindergarten are expected to use imaginary play skills at recess, when doing a group project or acting out scenes, on Halloween, or maybe when working with a social skills therapist. These are times you may practice pretending to be someone else.

b. When a student goes to school, teachers and everyone else know the person is a student, just like all the other kids at school. Other students get confused if another student comes to school and tells everyone that today he's a cowboy or a movie star, unless the student says, "Today I'm pretending to be a _____." When a student says he's pretending, people know he's just imagining what it must feel like to have one of these special jobs.

c. The best way to defeat Mr. Whoemeye is to enjoy yourself now. Your enjoyment will make it easier for you to feel more capable!

Mr. Whoemeye

CHAPTER 5
Introducing 14 New Thinkables

This chapter describes new Thinkables, all created by Social Town citizens. To learn more about Thinkables, the Very Cool Five-Step Power Plan, and more, see chapters 1 and 2. For expanded teacher materials about many of these Thinkables and for the image files for each of the chapter's illustrations, see the CD.

Wow! Clutter Buster

wants to give your brain superflexible, super organized power!

Power #1: **The Decider** power helps you to **stop, describe,** and **decide** the powers of the Thinkable.

- **Clutter Buster** gets people to be okay with making a plan and sticking to it to keep their things organized.

Power #2: The Social Detective power helps you to **observe** the situation and the people in the situation.

Clutter Buster

- Your Social Detective observes that most citizens start to develop some clutter piles around them but then the clutter gets in the way. "Clutter" means the things that pile up and make a mess around us. Clutter Buster helps with cleaning up these messy piles.

Power #3: The Brakester power helps you to **stop** and **think** to discover the hidden rules.

- When you notice things starting to pile up on your desk or in your room, Clutter Buster makes you stop and think about what you need to do with the things. Clutter Buster also helps you to figure out how long it will take to get your things organized and when you can do it.
- Figuring out how long it takes to organize your things takes practice, but citizens often find that it takes very little time to actually put away a paper (60 seconds?) or make a pile of their books so they're not spread out everywhere (maybe 30 seconds?).

Power #4: The Flex Do-Body power helps you to **use flexible thinking** to choose strategies to use **to do** what's expected.

a. Use checklists or schedules to remind yourself to take the time to clean up your space and use the powers of Clutter Buster!
b. If you're not sure when you can take the time to get organized, talk to your teacher or parent about their ideas for when you can do this.
c. Make a sticky note to remind yourself to take the time to bust your clutter!
d. If you'll put something away, decide on the best place to put it so you'll remember where it is. If you decide to throw something away or recycle it but aren't sure if it's okay, ask a parent or teacher first.

Power #5: The Cranium Coach power helps remind you to **use your self-talk** to tell yourself you've done well using new strategies.

- You can tell you've done this today when you can say to yourself:
"When I bust my clutter, it helps my brain be free of clutter too. This helps me focus on what I need to do and when I need to do it! Getting things done helps me feel good about myself."

Wow! Rainbow Girl

wants to give your brain superflexible, super organized power!

Power #1: **The Decider** power helps you to **stop, describe,** and **decide** the powers of the Thinkable.

- **Rainbow Girl** teaches people how to stay calm when something goes wrong. This helps them feel better in tough situations. The Unthinkables Rainbow Girl works to defeat include Emotion Commotion, Hurtful Harry, Icky Vicky, Mood Keeper, Past Willy, Rainstorm, and Negasorus Nix.

Power #2: **The Social Detective** power helps you to **observe** the situation and the people in the situation.

- Your Social Detective can observe not only what's going on with others but can also help you observe what it feels like inside of you. Being aware of your emotions and getting in control of how you react to those emotions can be some of the harder things you and all citizens have to learn.

Rainbow Girl

Power #3: **The Brakester** power helps you to **stop** and **think** to discover the hidden rules.

- As citizens grow up, they should develop more awareness of their emotions — how they feel at any given time and why they feel that way.
- Once your Social Detective has helped you to detect your emotions, your detective powers will also help you to stop and think about what you can do because of the way you're feeling. Rainbow Girl can help you find ways to calm down your thoughts, relax your body, and help you talk with others to do better at solving your problems.

Power #4: **The Flex Do-Body** power helps you to **use flexible thinking** to choose strategies to use **to do** what's expected.

a. Work with an adult to learn to identify your emotions and handle situations in which you get upset in a different way.
b. Use strategies to calm yourself, such as counting to 10 or taking deep breaths, breathing in through your nose and breathing out through your mouth.
c. Talk to a parent or teacher to find a quiet place to take a brain break if your brain gets stuck on upset.
d. Work at learning to think about some positive things in your life, even in difficult moments.

Power #5: **The Cranium Coach** power helps remind you to **use your self-talk** to tell yourself you've done well using new strategies.

- You can tell you've done this today when you can say to yourself: "I've learned ways in which I can help myself to stay calm even during difficult moments!"

Wow! Freezer Crystal
wants to give your brain superflexible, super organized power!

Powers of this Thinkable

- Brakester's relative **Freezer Crystal** causes people to STOP (freeze) and think about what they should do or how they should behave.

- Freezer Crystal lends a hand to Brakester to help you freeze your thinking for an instant to help you stop and think about what your Social Detective has noticed. This allows you to get your brain organized so you can figure out which superflexible strategies to use to defeat an Unthinkable.

- Your Social Detective will figure out the situation first and then Brakester and Freezer Crystal can jump in and help out!

Freezer Crystal

To do what's expected, use these Superflex strategies:

a. When your Social Detective notices the situation and you're about to do something that's unexpected or make a not-so-good choice, stop and visualize ice forming over your body. This will freeze you for a second while you think of hidden rules and expected ways to respond.

b. Once you FREEZE your actions, you can stop and think. This helps you get your superflexible thinking organized, see your choices, and figure out what might happen next depending on the choice you pick. This is also called trying to imagine the consequences. Looking at the consequences helps you to see which choice is the best choice to try to do what's expected. This helps you avoid having big problems.

Wow! Meditation Matt
wants to give your brain superflexible, super organized power!

Powers of this Thinkable

- **Meditation Matt** reminds citizens that before they can use their superflexible thinking, they have to be calm. This helps them to stop and think about good choices. When people are upset or angry, they need to use meditation or other ways to calm down before their Social Detective and Brakester powers can work very well.

To do what's expected, use these Superflex strategies:

a. Keep learning to notice how you feel. When you're angry, upset, or frustrated, you can learn how to calm down so that you can then use good strong superflexible thinking.

GETTING AND STAYING CALM: FREEZER CRYSTAL, MEDITATION MATT
CHAPTER 5 © 2012 SOCIAL THINKING PUBLISHING

b. To help calm down your thoughts, start by trying to calm down your body. One way is to use some some deep breathing. Some people even do some meditation (like Matt). Meditation is a way to relax and become calm by using the powers of your brain to calm down your body. People usually close their eyes and really focus their thinking on something when they meditate. They try hard not to think about their worries or about what people might be doing around them.

People meditate in different ways — for example, some citizens think to themselves one word over and over and others focus on listening to their breaths. Your parents or teachers may have more information on who in your Social Town can teach you about meditation.

c. Your parent or teacher may also want to use a book called *The Zones of Regulation* (Kuypers, 2011) to help teach you more ways that your body and brain can work together to help you use superflexible thinking!

Meditation Matt

Wow! Please Activate Waiting System (P.A.W.S.)

wants to give your brain superflexible, super organized power!

Powers of this Thinkable

- The **Please Activate Waiting System,** called **P.A.W.S.** for short, helps people remember to wait before reacting to things that happen. PAWS is a Thinkable who acts as an advisor to Brakester and is in the same family with Freezer Crystal and Meditation Matt.

Please Activate Waiting System (P.A.W.S.)

To do what's expected, use these Superflex strategies:

a. Remember that you can P.A.W.S. — or PAUSE — and think things over before you react. This often helps you be more flexible.

b. P.A.W.S. helps as you use Brakester. This is the system Brakester uses to help put on the brakes!

Wow! Space Respecter

wants to give your brain superflexible, super organized power!

Space Respecter

Power #1: The **Decider** power helps you to **stop, describe,** and **decide** the powers of the Thinkable.

- **Space Respecter** helps people to be mindful of others' personal space and to stay out of their space bubbles.

Power #2: The **Social Detective** power helps you to **observe** the situation and the people in the situation.

- Your Social Detective sees that the distance people stand apart from each other is based on the situation and the people in the situation.

Power #3: The **Brakester** power helps you to **stop** and **think** to discover the hidden rules.

- People figure out how far away or how close they should be to other people mostly based on if they want to talk with them or not. People can figure out this distance with an "imaginary space bubble locator" because everyone likes to have a bit of a space bubble around them.
- When citizens are just standing around, they often stand at least two arms' length away from each other. If they plan to talk with each other, they usually stand about one arm's length away from another person. In really crowded places like an elevator, people often need to stand closer to each other even when they don't plan to talk.
- Citizens feel comfortable when other citizens are able to keep an expected space bubble around people they're talking or hanging out with.

Power #4: The **Flex Do-Body** power helps you to **use flexible thinking** to choose strategies to use **to do** what's expected.

a. Use your Social Detective powers to observe how far away you and other people are standing from each other in a situation.
b. Help Space Respecter defeat Space Invader by using the fantastic powers of the space bubble locator. Move away from people or closer to them if needed.
c. If a person asks you to move away from him, maybe by giving you a slight nudge on your back, shoulder, or arm, put Space Respecter into high gear. Quickly move out of that person's space and keep Space Respecter on a high setting.

Power #5: The **Cranium Coach** power helps remind you to **use your self-talk** to tell yourself you've done well using new strategies.

- You can tell you've done this today when you can say to yourself:
  "I used my space bubble locator well because people know I'm standing near them when I want to talk with them and they know when I'm not planning to speak."

CHAPTER 5 © 2012 SOCIAL THINKING PUBLISHING

Wow! Space Raptor
wants to give your brain superflexible, super organized power!

Powers of this Thinkable

- **Space Raptor** specializes in helping people be aware of how they share the space they are in with others! Space Raptor helps citizens think about body language and what their bodies are saying when they are talking to others so citizens look friendlier.

To do what's expected, use these Superflex strategies:

Space Raptor

a. Remind yourself to think with your eyes, look toward people you are talking to, which will help you keep your head up when you're out walking around or hanging out.

b. You can use the saying "Nose over toes" to help you keep looking up and observing what's around you. You can also think about pointing your toes and shoulders toward the group of people you're with or toward the person speaking. When you do these things, people will think you are interested in being with them which means you also look friendlier! Being thought of as friendly helps you feel better about yourself as well!

Wow! Captain Choice
wants to give your brainsuperflexible, super organized power!

Captain Choice

Power #1: The **Decider** power helps you to **stop, describe,** and **decide** the powers of the Thinkable.

- **Captain Choice** helps people think about what choices they have and how they can make a choice quickly to keep going with all the things they need to do in a day!

Power #2: The **Social Detective** power helps you to **observe** the situation and the people in the situation.

- Your Social Detective helps you see that citizens all around you are making choices. When children make a choice, they know that their choice won't last a long time (the game they chose will end, the food they chose will get eaten, etc.). When people know they're not stuck with their choice forever, it helps them stay calm even when they don't like their choice.

Power #3: The **Brakester** power helps you to **stop** and **think** to discover the hidden rules.

- If you're not able to see the choices you have, an adult may help you to figure out your choices by showing them to you or writing them down in a list. Once you see your choices, it's expected that you'll be able to make your choice quickly. The choice you make doesn't have to mean you love the choice or are excited about it but your choices will help you get through your day.

Power #4: The **Flex Do-Body** power helps you to **use flexible thinking** to choose strategies to use **to do** what's expected.

- Here are some things you can do to help you learn to make choices:
  a. Notice your different choices. An adult can help you with this.
  b. When making the choice, stay calm and remember your choice isn't permanent!
  c. Make your choice within about 10–20 seconds.
  d. As you experience the choice you've made, think about the new experience you may be having and learning from.
  e. Be proud of yourself if you were able to do all of these steps because Captain Choice has guided your thinking and your Superflex is becoming more powerful!

Power #5: The **Cranium Coach** power helps remind you to **use your self-talk** to tell yourself you've done well using new strategies.

- You can tell you've done this today when you can say to yourself:
  "I noticed my choices, made a quick choice, and stayed calm throughout the whole process. That means my Captain Choice is helping me do a really good job!"

MAKING CHOICES: CAPTAIN CHOICE
CHAPTER 5 © 2012 SOCIAL THINKING PUBLISHING

Wow! Focus Tron
wants to give your brain superflexible, super organized power!

Power #1: **The Decider** power helps you to **stop, describe,** and **decide** the powers of the Thinkable.

- This Thinkable helps people defeat Brain Eater, Day Dreamer, One-Sided Sid, Body Snatcher, and Energy Hare-y. **Focus Tron** gives people greater focusing powers.

Power #2: **The Social Detective** power helps you to **observe** the situation and the people in the situation.

- Your Social Detective notices when citizens look like they can't focus on what they're supposed to be doing. One clue is that people's eyes seem to be looking at something different than their work or the person speaking.

Focus Tron

Power #3: **The Brakester** power helps you to **stop** and **think** to discover the hidden rules.

- If people find they're getting very distracted and can't focus, they first need to notice that one of the Unthinkables is trying to gain power in their mind! Next, they should stop and think about ways to help themselves pay attention again — using help from Focus Tron. Then they can focus on what they need to do or what's expected.

Power #4: **The Flex Do-Body** power helps you to **use flexible thinking** to choose strategies to use **to do** what's expected.

a. Try and remember to think with your eyes about what the speaker is telling the group.
b. Keep your hands busy by touching or squeezing a fidget, an object like Silly Putty or a squishy ball. This is a Focus Tron way to help you keep your brain focused on your work. IMPORTANT NOTE: If you're using a fidget but you start focusing on your fidget, the fidget is now a distracter. Distracters are taken away because they're not helping to sharpen your Focus Tron!
c. Move to a quieter place to work in the classroom.
d. Find a different way to sit in the classroom to make it easier for your body to let your brain focus. This could be with an exercise ball or a beanbag chair.
e. An occupational therapist (a special teacher at school) can help you choose which of these strategies will help give your Focus Tron more power to help defeat the Unthinkables.

Power #5: **The Cranium Coach** power helps remind you to **use your self-talk** to tell yourself you've done well using new strategies.

- You can tell you've done this today when you can say to yourself:
"I used my eyes and body well to help my brain concentrate (focus) on what I'm supposed to be doing!"

Wow! Tim Taskstick-Able
wants to give your brain superflexible, super organized power!

Powers of this Thinkable

- **Tim Taskstick-Able** is a real "doer" who helps people be able to start and complete a task. This Thinkable defeats Brain Eater by using the powers of concentration and working hard.

To do what's expected, use these Superflex strategies:

a. Think about what you're supposed to be doing.

b. Thinks about ways in which Tim Taskstick-Able can help you adjust your body so it's easier for you to continue to pay attention.

c. Use your inner coach to remind you that you'll only have to spend a little bit of time on this task to complete it.

d. Use your self-talk to tell yourself you're doing well concentrating and working through the task rather than taking the time to complain about it.

Tim Taskstick-Able

Wow! Inventor of Fun (I.O.F.)
wants to give your brain superflexible, super organized power!

Power #1: **The Decider** power helps you to **stop, describe,** and **decide** the powers of the Thinkable.

Inventor of Fun (I.O.F.)

- **Inventor of Fun (I.O.F.)** helps people have fun and cooperate with others during sports and other games. This Thinkable defeats D.O.F. Destroyer of Fun, by helping people to be good sports and use friendly words with others they're playing with, even players on the other team.
- I.O.F. also gives people the power to stay positive and let little things go during a game, like if they mess up a play during a game.

Power #2: The Social Detective power helps you to **observe** the situation and the people in the situation.

- Your Social Detective notices how people try to keep other citizens feeling good while they're playing sports and other games together. They make friendly comments and might let others go first or not seem upset if they don't get to go first. But your detective may also see how people start to get frustrated or stop having a good time when other people are poor sports or are negative and mean to each other.

Power #3: The Brakester power helps you to **stop** and **think** to discover the hidden rules.

- When you play with others, it's expected to remember the hidden rules for the game you're playing so everyone can have a fun time. It's also expected that everyone uses friendly and helpful words to show others that they enjoy playing with them.

Power #4: The Flex Do-Body power helps you to **use flexible thinking** to choose strategies to use **to do** what's expected.

a. Continue to think about how much fun you and others have when you're being fair and cooperative when you play.
b. Use your inner coach to help you think positively when the game may not be going your way. You can think to yourself: "Winning and going first isn't everything, and I'm still having fun with my teammates."
c. Learn more about different sizes of problems, from tiny problems to huge (earthquake-sized) ones. This will help make it easier for you to notice problems when you play with others and think about how most of them are tiny.

Power #5: The Cranium Coach power helps remind you to **use your self-talk** to tell yourself you've done well using new strategies.

- You can tell you've done this today when you can say to yourself:
"I'm having fun playing games and being part of sports teams. My friends and other people I play with are having a good time and enjoying themselves."

Wow! Sunny Sun
wants to give your brain superflexible, super organized power!

Power #1: **The Decider** power helps you to **stop, describe,** and **decide** the powers of the Thinkable.

- **Sunny Sun** helps people see all the good things in a day and to feel pretty good about their lives. People who can do this are described as having a really positive attitude. People can defeat Grump Grumpaniny and Dark Defeatist with Sunny Sun's amazing powers of positive thinking and talking.

Power #2: **The Social Detective** power helps you to **observe** the situation and the people in the situation.

- Your Social Detective notices that some citizens have pretty good attitudes even when they don't love doing what they have to do! Most people look relaxed and happy when things are going well. When things get hard to deal with, some people are grumpy and upset and think they won't succeed.

Sunny Sun

Power #3: **The Brakester** power helps you to **stop** and **think** to discover the hidden rules.

- When citizens have to do something they don't like, they usually do better at getting through the work if they have a good attitude (the power of Sunny Sun) rather than a bad attitude (Grump Grumpaniny).

Power #4: **The Flex Do-Body** power helps you to **use flexible thinking** to choose strategies to use **to do** what's expected.

- Use your inner coach to help you stay focused and more positive about something you have to do. Here are some things your inner coach can say:
  a. "I can do the work."
  b. "This won't take all my time. If I break up this task into smaller parts, I can be proud of myself for doing each part I get done."
  c. "I'll focus on how good I'll feel when I finish this."
  d. "I can talk to others in a more bright and cheerful way. I then can also be proud of myself for staying pleasant when I have to do something I don't like to do."

Power #5: **The Cranium Coach** power helps remind you to **use your self-talk** to tell yourself you've done well using new strategies.

- You can tell you've done this today when you can say to yourself:
  "I stayed pretty calm and friendly while also focused on tasks I don't like to do."

POSITIVE ATTITUDE: SUNNY SUN

Wow! Dino Thinker
wants to give your brain superflexible, super organized power!

Power #1: **The Decider** power helps you to **stop, describe,** and **decide** the powers of the Thinkable.

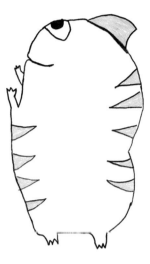

Dino Thinker

- **Dino Thinker** chews away and gets rid of bad thoughts that might invade people's brains during the day by helping them think positive thoughts. With Dino Thinker around, people remember their minds are as big and strong as a dinosaur and that they can overcome their bad thoughts.

Power #2: **The Social Detective** power helps you to **observe** the situation and the people in the situation.

- Your Social Detective notices that people can often limit the negative thoughts that can take over a brain throughout the day. You often don't even notice when others might be having negative thoughts because they're so good at moving through the negative moment and not showing it on the outside.

Power #3: **The Brakester** power helps you to **stop** and **think** to discover the hidden rules.

- All citizens have to battle negative thoughts, but it's expected that they take time to think about how to push these thoughts out of their brains before they cause a problem. If people get too many negative thoughts in their brain that they can't defeat, they can start to feel pretty bad about themselves. Citizens know that the better they feel about themselves, the more positive thoughts they can fill their brains with.

Power #4: **The Flex Do-Body** power helps you to **use flexible thinking** to choose strategies to use **to do** what's expected.

a. Notice when your thoughts start to get negative and are making it hard for you to get through things like your schoolwork or a new activity. Call on Dino Thinker to focus your thoughts on good things you can look forward to, rather than getting stuck on thinking about what you don't like to do.

b. Write or draw a picture of your negative thought, crumble up the paper, and throw the thought in the trash to get rid of it. Draw a picture of something you'll get to do later that you enjoy.

c. Use your inner coach to remind yourself that you're big and strong like a dinosaur and can defeat those negative thoughts!

Power #5: **The Cranium Coach** power helps remind you to **use your self-talk** to tell yourself you've done well using new strategies.

- You can tell you've done this today when you can say to yourself: "I've been able to feel more positive about myself and who I am. I know I can get through things that are tough when I focus on more positive thoughts in my brain!"

Wow! Wings

wants to give your brain superflexible, super organized power!

Power #1: **The Decider** power helps you to **stop, describe,** and **decide** the powers of the Thinkable.

- **Wings** is based on the scientific theory called the "butterfly effect." Scientists say that when a butterfly flaps her wings, small changes happen in the air around the butterfly that lead to other changes in the air. These in time become part of something much bigger.
- Wings uses her wings to make kindness grow. Wings wants Superflex kids to think of something kind to do or say each day.

Wings

Power #2: **The Social Detective** power helps you to **observe** the situation and the people in the situation.

- Your Social Detective notices that when someone treats other citizens well, those citizens tend to respond by treating others well. As people treat others well, each of their Wings gains power and the butterfly effect is working!

Power #3: **The Brakester** power helps you to **stop** and **think** to discover the hidden rules.

- People who are thought of as kind are likely to follow a variety of hidden rules, such as stepping out of the way to let someone pass in the hall, offering help when they see someone needs it, standing up against a fellow student who may be bullying or being mean to another citizen, showing interest in what a person is talking about, and working hard to try and do what teachers ask for in class.

Power #4: **The Flex Do-Body** power helps you to **use flexible thinking** to choose strategies to use **to do** what's expected.

a. Brainstorm a list of other actions people can do that use Wings' power to show kindness to others.
b. Work at performing at least one small act of kindness each day, if not many more!
c. Notice when others do something nice and respond to it in a positive manner.
d. Keep unkind thoughts and actions to yourself.

Power #5: **The Cranium Coach** power helps remind you to **use your self-talk** to tell yourself you've done well using new strategies.

- You can tell you've done this today when you can say to yourself:
"I notice that I'm doing things and saying things that make others feel good. It makes me happy to sprout my Wings because I'm helping to make the world a better place to live."

SPREADING KINDNESS: WINGS

CHAPTER 6
About the Contributors

Many citizens of Social Town helped create the new Unthinkables and Thinkables that appear in this book. Let's give them all a big thumbs up and thanks!

Antsy Nancy (Page 70)

Lisa Carter, EdS, NCSP
Lisa is a school psychologist living in Odenton, Maryland. A Virginia Tech and Radford University graduate, Lisa also earned a post-baccalaureate certificate in Autism Studies. Like many members of Social Town, she battles several of the Unthinkables in her personal life alongside the students she works with.

Armored Alex (Page 66)

Bobbi Leier, school counselor
Shanna Crouse, speech language pathologist
Shanna and Bobbi co-teach the Superflex group at Roosevelt Elementary. They enjoy facilitating this dynamic group of students and look forward to watching the students work toward improved social and positive thinking skills each week.

Students: Natalie Edwards, fifth grade, and Declan J., fourth grade
Natalie loves dogs and learning facts about the United States.

Declan is ten years old and likes jetpacks, going to the farm, and exploring. Declan decided to use an armadillo in his drawing to show how people sometimes get frustrated and hide in their shells, just like an armadillo does when it's afraid.

Attention Eater (Page 39)

Becky Fukuda, paraeducator
Becky is a paraprofessional in a self-contained special education classroom for fourth, fifth, and sixth graders in Kenmore, Washington. A former lawyer, she left that profession to work for an education nonprofit. When she had her first child, she left her job and started volunteering and then substitute teaching at her neighborhood school. After she subbed in a special education classroom, she was hooked and has been a classroom assistant ever since.

Bedman (Page 105)

Carrie Moberg, special education teacher
Julie Samuelson
Student: Antoine Johnson, Jr., fourth grade

ABOUT THE CONTRIBUTORS

Big Bubble Bob (Page 97)

Marsha B. Schoene-Langohr, teacher

Marsha has been a resource room special education teacher at Thornton Creek Elementary School for 21 years. She started having the students draw and write about their own Unthinkables and Thinkables three years ago. They made these into their own books for the students and school library. Marsha got inspired to start this because the students kept thinking of new Unthinkables as they discussed the ones from Superflex. Some students then decided they wanted to make up Thinkables, so they did and continue to do this every year.

Student: Russell C., third grade

Russell is a student at Thornton Creek and is nine years old. He likes drawing and has drawn a lot of pictures.

Blurt Out Blue (Page 42)

Shannon Gasiorowski, kindergarten teacher

Shannon teaches at Kennedy Elementary School in Grafton, Wisconsin. Kennedy School was introduced to Social Town, Superflex, and the Unthinkables through skits, all-school assemblies, and stories. Shannon came up with the Unthinkable Blurt Out Blue when many of her students weren't raising their hands and instead were shouting out in class discussions. Her students came up with the name Blurt Out Blue and strategies to defeat this Unthinkable.

Mike Driscoll, art teacher

Mike worked with the kindergarten class and designed the look of Blurt Out Blue.

Sheila Binder, school psychologist

Blurt Out Blue is used in the schoolwide Superflex program. Students relate well to this Unthinkable and interruptions have decreased. Thanks Superflex!

Boastful Bore (Page 43)

Nancy Weiss, speech language pathologist

Boastful Bore was created in a social skills program following a brainstorming activity about types of people who aren't social thinkers. Together the boys said that they don't like kids who only talk about themselves; it makes them "bored."

Students: Michael Bunt, fifth grade, and Andrew Vavricka, sixth grade

Book Magnet (Page 87)

The Parish School teachers
The teachers found this Unthinkable when they noticed so many of their students kept disappearing to read books instead of doing homework, listening, or even staying in the group. It was like a magnet was just pulling them away. The teachers understood, but it was definitely causing problems for them in getting their work done or paying attention to other students. Look up the Parish School at www.parishschool.org.

Student: Austin Cowden, third grader
Austin, who is eight years old, drew the picture for Book Magnet.

Bored Bobby (Page 69)

Ryan Hendrix, MS, CCC-SLP
Ryan is a social cognitive therapist in the San Francisco Bay Area and part of the Social Thinking-Stevens Creek team.

Student: Zachary Brugger, fifth grade
Zachary writes that he's creative and funny and likes defeating Unthinkables. His tutor Ryan inspired him to create these Unthinkables: Bored Bobby, who overwhelms him with boredom, La-Ti-Da, who makes him hum at unexpected times, and Munchie Munchie, who makes him eat when he shouldn't. Go Superflex!

Brakester (Page 15)

Ginny Thompson, MS, CCC-SLP
Ginny serves Perry Harrison School and functions as the speech language pathologist on the district's autism team. She completed Michelle Garcia Winner's mentor training program in 2008. Her greatest joy and passion is helping individuals with social thinking differences navigate our very complex world.

ABOUT THE CONTRIBUTORS
CHAPTER 6 © 2012 SOCIAL THINKING PUBLISHING

Can't Be Wrong Rita (Page 82)

Clare Fuller, speech language pathologist

Student: Kaya Morrison, sixth grade

Clare is a speech language pathologist and psychotherapist in Vancouver who has her own practice called SocialWorks. Kaya developed Can't Be Wrong Rita and Clare and Kaya created the strategies together to overcome her. Can't Be Wrong Rita was created because sometimes people have difficulty when they don't know something or have the information wrong. Clare and Kaya decided it would be helpful to have an Unthinkable who gets in your head and makes you stuck on the idea that you have to be right!

Captain Blame-O (Page 95)

Amy Davenport, school counselor

Jed Davenport, director of the Midland Adult Probation Department

Amy is an elementary school counselor in Midland, Texas who conducts weekly small groups based on Superflex curriculum to help children with social skills deficits. Amy is also the proud mother of two young children who are quite familiar with Superflex vocabulary. The Unthinkable Captain Blame-O was created by her husband Jed who came to the realization that many people blame others for their behaviors and/or choices, rather than accept responsibility for them.

Captain Choice (Page 116)

Sherry C. Mergner, MSW, LCSW

Sherry is a clinical assistant professor at the University of North Carolina at Chapel Hill School of Social Work where she coordinates continuing education programs for mental health professionals. She is the proud mother of Noah, 13 years old with high-functioning autism, and Nathan, 9 years old, who is typically developing. Sherry is very active in her community and within her children's school promoting autism awareness and education. Noah has provided much inspiration for Sherry's work in the autism field.

Student: Noah Hrynewych, sixth grade

Noah has high-functioning autism and is a student at Hawbridge Charter School in Saxawpaw, North Carolina. He's a lover of trains, music, and slapstick. He wants to be a train engineer when he grows up.

Clutter Buster (Page 110)

Janine Kessler, speech language pathologist

Janine is a speech language pathologist (as well as a wife and mother of three amazing kids). She and Benjamin learned the Superflex program together when he was in first grade. They love Social Town.

Student: Benjamin David Weiler, second grade

When Benjamin was in first grade, he came up with the idea to create a new Thinkable named Clutter Buster who helped him keep his desk organized. Benjamin likes to play on the computer and to write books about a character named Macho Nacho who is another superhero.

Collider (Page 72)

Ginny Thompson, MS, CCC-SLP

See "Brakester" to learn more about Ginny.

Student: Zachary B.

Concrete Connie (Page 77

Diane Lewis, MA, CCC-SLP

Diane is a speech language pathologist who is the founder and director of Children's Innovative Therapy Group, LLC (CITG). She is the coauthor with Stanley I. Greenspan, MD, of *The Affect-Based Language Curriculum (ABLC) — An Intensive Program for Families, Therapists and Teachers* (2nd edition, 2005). She has extensive experience working with children on the autism spectrum.

Student: Elias Tsakiris, eighth grade

Elias, who is now fourteen years old, has been seeing Ms. Lewis since he was two and a half. At that time, he was nonverbal and had severe auditory processing difficulties. He now attends High

Road Academy, has a second-degree black belt, and plays defense on his hockey team. A few months ago he commented about the Unthinkables and said: "Why are all the Unthinkables negative?" This is how this journey of creating Thinkables and Unthinkables began.

Confusion Carol (Page 62)

Deanna Rozak, speech language pathologist

Student: Erica Cerasale, fourth grade
Deanna is a speech language pathologist who works in an elementary school in Prospect, Connecticut. Confusion Carol was created by one of her students in the course of writing a cartoon about an experience that she had had in school. They attempted to apply her emotional state to an Unthinkable character and found that there was no character for that situation. Deanna asked if Erica could create one that would work and she did!

Copy Cat (Page 40)

Lara Feldman, child therapist
Lara is a registered social worker and registered clinical counselor who works with children providing play therapy and social cognitive therapy. Her approach with children is nondirective and therefore child led. Konrad created the Unthinkable Copy Cat and Ethan created Igor Interrupter. Lara facilitated by helping them to form clear concepts during their social group at Victoria Group Perspectives Therapy Services.

Student: Konrad Loy, fifth grade
Konrad worked with a fellow student on developing Unthinkables for this competition. Konrad had noticed that kids often copy other kids to annoy them or be funny. He realized that kids don't like it when someone copies them and that it makes them uncomfortable. He decided to create Copy Cat. Konrad attends a weekly Social Thinking group at Victoria Group Perspectives Therapy Services.

Danger Dave (Page 47)

Alicia Walker, occupational therapist
Alicia is a pediatric occupational therapist who works at Children's

Therapy Associates in Natick, Massachusetts. Danger Dave was inspired by many of the kids who attend individual occupational therapy and The Social Adventure Group Program, co-led by Speech and OT. Danger Dave tends to leap before he looks and frequently moves so quickly he forgets to check in about his safety and the safety of others.

Student: Abigael Drake, second grade

Dark Defeatist (Page 65)

Becky Fukuda, paraeducator
See "Attention Eater" to learn more about Becky.

Dino Thinker (Page 121)

Carrie Moberg, special education teacher

Students: Pete S., third grade, Jake A. Guerrero, fifth grade
Jake loves drawing different types of creatures. Dino Thinker was inspired by his classmate who gave Jake encouragement about his artistic abilities and his passion for dinosaurs.

Disappointed Dan (Page 66)

Glenna Clouse, MEd, LMHC

Student: Hadley Nyberg, sixth grade
Glenna is a licensed mental health counselor at Puget Sound Counseling and Autism Services. The students in her social learning groups absolutely love Superflex and all that comes with him. They started creating their own characters two years ago. When the contest came along, the kids were inspired even more.

Dr. Downloader (Page 100)

Kari Palmer, social cognitive therapist
Kari is a social cognitive therapist and consultant whose private practice, Changing Perspectives, is based in Excelsior, Minnesota. Dr. Downloader found his way into many of her sessions, especially related to topics of computers, video games, natural disasters, Star Wars, and war tactics.

ABOUT THE CONTRIBUTORS

To create a comfortable space to talk about "downloading" (providing more information than others want to hear about a particular topic), this Unthinkable was created.

Student: Thomas Lane, third grade

Dream Catcher (Page 104)

Renee Tompkins, speech language pathologist
Renee, a speech language pathologist in the Poway Unified School District, works at the Transition Program with adults from 18 to 22 years old. The Unthinkables have been a huge success with all of her students and staff.

Student: Shaun T. Bridges, student, age 22
Shaun is a student in the Poway Unified School District's Transition Program. Shaun created Dream Catcher because he noticed that one of his peers was falling asleep during speech group. He knew that was an unexpected behavior and wanted to develop a new Unthinkable to address the behavior.

Egg-Certain (Page 86)

Carrie Moberg, special education teacher
Student: Sam Judge, fifth grade

Emotion Commotion (Page 49)

The Mayor and Town Council of Social Town: Stephanie Madrigal, Michelle Garcia Winner, and Pam Crooke.
See The Social Town Book Committee at the end of this chapter and www.socialthinking.com to learn more about them.

Empathy Eraser (Page 78)

Melinda Wernke, school psychologist
Melinda helped J.R. come up with ideas to sketch out the Empathy Eraser, a character that he independently thought up after learning about this opportunity. Melinda is a school psychologist in Douglas County School District, Colorado.

Student: J.R., sixth grade

J., a student at Heritage Elementary, reports that the Empathy Eraser is the Unthinkable that most often invades his brain, getting rid of empathy and making him think only of himself. He hopes to make this huge problem known and to give students strategies to help them defeat this Unthinkable.

Falsificator (Page 94)

Becky Fukuda, paraeducator
See "Attention Eater" to learn more about Becky.

Fear Releaser (Page 48)

Valerie Kenyon, speech language pathologist
Valerie works at Mendon Center Elementary School of Pittsford, New York. With her support and that of Kathryn, one of the school counselors, fifth grade student Alex created Fear Releaser to help with identifying and overcoming his fear of walking in the school hallways as well as other fears he was encountering in and out of school. Alex really connected to the idea of Superflex and the Unthinkables and was further motivated by his ability to create and defeat his own Unthinkable.

Kathryn Borden, school counselor
Student: Alex Krebs, fifth grade

First Fighter (Page 44)

Amanda Wenrich, itinerant autism support teacher
Michael and Amanda developed First Fighter to help Michael cope with not always being first. By using the superflexible strategies, Michael has learned to stay calm and remember that he can be first another time. Michael loves defeating First Fighter.

Student: Michael Sweitzer, fifth grade
Michael, a student at Cornwall Elementary School in Cornwall, Pennsylvania, enjoys learning about the Superflex characters with his itinerant autism support teacher, Mrs. Amanda Wenrich. Michael's favorite school subject is social studies and he loves Mack trucks. Michael lives with his parents, sister, and two cats.

ABOUT THE CONTRIBUTORS
CHAPTER 6 © 2012 SOCIAL THINKING PUBLISHING

Focus Tron (Page 117)

Jamie Gibson, child and youth counselor
D. Brad Gibson, artist for Focus Tron

Students: Jacob Subject, Gregg, and Cole Langlois
Focus Tron was created by a group of fifth grade students at Campbell River Christian School. The Superflex program has helped them be aware of how their actions influence others and how to combat those pesky Unthinkables! Focus Tron was developed to help them remain focused in classroom and social situations.

Freezer Crystal (Page 112)

Glenna Clouse, MEd, LMHC
See "Disappointed Dan" to learn more about Glenna.

Student: Seth Olson, seventh grade
Seth first learned about Superflex and the team of Unthinkables when he was in fifth grade and has done a great job of using strategies to defeat Unthinkables. But, as he has stated, sometimes he just needs to stop instantly and think about his next move. That's why he invented Freezer Crystal.

Garbage Can Crew (Page 90)

Deborah Finkelstein, NCC, LCPC
A graduate of Loyala University in Maryland's School Counseling Program, Deborah has been a school counselor in Howard County, Maryland for five years. The students at Running Brook Elementary love the Superflex program and are always inspiring her to come up with new Unthinkable characters.

Get in Trouble Man (Page 40)

Marsha B. Schoene-Langohr, teacher
See "Big Bubble Bob" to learn more about Marsha.

Student: Charlie Funk, fifth grade
Charlie was a fourth grade student at Thornton Creek Elementary School in Seattle, Washington when he created Get in Trouble Man. Charlie sometimes gets in trouble in class because he's very

social and a bit of a clown. He loves soccer, baseball, and the arts, particularly singing and drawing.

Hermit Crab (Page 88)

Jacqueline Guers, teacher/ABA tutor
Jacqueline is extremely proud of Jordan for all the hard work he put in designing and creating his Unthinkable. She has been Jordan's ABA tutor for over a year. She's also employed as an elementary teacher for the Deaf. Jordan loved reading about Superflex battling the Unthinkables, and Jacqueline enjoyed using the Superflex curriculum with him.

Student: Jordan Ware, fourth grade
Jordan is a Pokémon expert and is nine years old. He created the Unthinkable Hermit Crab because he likes to play video games. Hermit Crab is an Unthinkable who wants people to sit at home and play video games all day long and not socialize with others.

Holiday Boulder (Page 55)

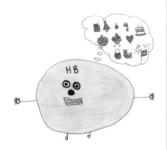

Ginny Thompson, MS, CCC-SLP
See "Brakester" to learn more about Ginny.

Student: Noah Hrynewych, sixth grade
See "Captain Choice" to learn more about Noah.

Hurtful Harry (Page 50)

Ginny Thompson, MS, CCC-SLP
See "Brakester" to learn more about Ginny.

Student: Noah Hrynewych
See "Captain Choice" to learn more about Noah.

Icky Vicky (Page 51)

Jaime Rivetts, MS Ed, social cognitive specialist
Jaime is the executive director of the Idaho Social Learning Center. Icky Vicky was inspired by the need for children to understand how to cope with and process negative thoughts that lead to a low self-esteem. Understanding Icky Vicky allows her students to

feel empowered and to have control over their own thoughts and feelings.

Students: Hennessey Star, fourth grade, and Maren Feltman, third grade

Hennessey and Maren were learning about the Unthinkables and both had this Unthinkable to battle. They don't battle her any more because they use their strategies to defeat her. It has helped them make more friends, feel good about themselves, and learn how to be better social thinkers.

Igor Interrupter (Page 73)

Angie Harasyn

Angie, Ethan's mom, came to be a member of Social Town through supporting her enthusiastic son's hard work at his Group Perspective sessions.

Lara Feldman, child therapist

See "Copy Cat" to learn more about Lara.

Student: Ethan Harasyn, fourth grade

Ethan is an active, sporty dude who enjoys football, hockey, basketball, Star Wars, LEGO, Wipeout, video games, NERF guns, and reading. He's also an avid conversationalist and came up with Igor Interrupter idea as a fun way to work on defeating this new Unthinkable.

Impatient Octopus (Page 71)

Beth Sardinha

Beth is proud to be Ava Sardinha's mother. She's Ava's biggest fan and supports her in all of her creative endeavors.

Student: Ava Sardinha, second grade

Ava is eight years and began Social Thinking sessions at the Autism Project in Johnston, Rhode Island in 2009. Ava likes reading, drawing, writing stories, and telling jokes. She loves animals and also enjoys music and singing. Ava created Impatient Octopus because her brain can get so busy, like an octopus with eight legs wanting to do a different job with each leg.

Information Station (Page 99)

Maureen E. McMullen, MS, CCC-SLP
Maureen is a speech language pathologist at Hamilton Elementary School, North Kingstown, Rhode Island.

Inspiration for this Unthinkable came from one of her elementary students who was moving up to the middle school. He had a wealth of information on every topic that his listeners had little patience for. Information Station was created to build his awareness so he could have a strategy handy to use while he conversed with peers.

Nancy Ciccone, special education paraprofessional, illustrator of Information Station

Int-Erupter (Page 73)

Audra Jensen, MEd, BCBA, director of Autism Behavioral Consulting
Int-Erupter and The Enforcer were developed in Social Thinking groups at Autism Behavioral Consulting in Vancouver, Washington. Students there enjoy coming together with ideas about new "evil villains," what they do, and how we can conquer them. They also enjoy giving ideas on how the Unthinkables should be illustrated. Information about ABC can be found at www.autismabc.org or email info@autismabc.org.

Debbie McCord, BA, BCaBA, program manager, illustrator of Int-Erupter
Debbie is one of the Autism Behavioral Consulting clinic's program managers and helped come up with the idea of new Unthinkables. With her background in illustration, she was able to design characters to look similar to the original Unthinkables, making them fit right into the "team."

Inter-Ruptor (Page 74)

Rebecca L. Hack, K-2 special education teacher
Rebecca has been teaching at Davenport Grade School in Eureka, Illinois since 1997. She became a member of Social Town in 2012 and loves teaching her students Social Thinking/Social Sense.

Inter-Ruptor and Tiny Teacher were created after seeing a need during her social language groups.

Tiffani Schmitt, school social worker
Tiffani has been a school social worker for 21 years. She became a citizen of Social Town in August 2010 and plans to take up permanent residency. Tiny Teacher and Inter-Ruptor were created during a Superflex Training Academy session.

Interruptagator (Page 75)

Penny Green, speech language pathologist
Penny specializes in working with preschool and elementary school aged children. Social Thinking groups take place in families' homes, providing opportunities for play and friendships. Parents and grandparents participate in groups and follow up on concepts at home, which encourages generalization and has been instrumental in helping children succeed.

Inventor of Fun (I.O.F.) (Page 119)

Deb Jensen, speech language pathologist
Deb has worked in the Minnetonka, Minnesota schools for the past 26 years and facilitated "social" groups at West Metro Learning Connections in Excelsior. She also works on call for Courage Center Burnsville.

Sandy Curry, school social worker
Sandy Curry has worked in the Minnetonka schools for the past 24 years and prior to that worked in a hospital setting at Metropolitan Medical Center in Minneapolis. She and Deb enjoy working together using Social Thinking Vocabulary and the Superflex curriculum.

Student: Cooper Sposito, third grade
Cooper is a student at Clear Springs Elementary School in Minnetonka. Cooper created his Thinkable character Inventor of Fun (I.O.F.) during his social skills group. Cooper loves to draw and is a creative thinker. He's familiar with the Superflex curriculum and knows the characters. The contest was a fun way for a student like Cooper to use his creativity, flexibility, and prior knowledge to develop his new Thinkable character.

Justice Buster (Page 55)

Jenny Moss, former special education teacher, current PhD student

Jenny Moss is a former teacher with experience at many levels, including special education. Currently she's a PhD student studying Human Development and Family Sciences at Oregon State University. She was introduced to Social Town by her daughter Annie and tries to be like Superflex as much as she can.

Student: Annie Moss, second grade

Annie lives in Oregon and enjoys thinking big thoughts, practicing Taekwondo, and singing. Annie made up an imaginary world of Bombar and tells stories about it. She thinks Social Town is a cool place to be and likes making up new residents, both Thinkables and Unthinkables.

Kenny Can't (Page 67)

Sara Enis, special education teacher

Sara teaches Resource Room and Social Skills for students on the autism spectrum at Central Elementary School in East Bruswick, New Jersey. She uses the Social Town Unthinkables daily in the classroom and developed this character with one of her students to target his frustration in the classroom setting.

Student: A.M.S., third grade

A. is a nine-year-old boy at Central Elementary School. He developed Kenny Can't to help him overcome his classroom frustrations and fear that the work is too hard. This character helps A. realize that he can be successful if he just puts in the effort and tries his best.

La-Ti-Da (Page 76)

Ryan Hendrix, MS, CCC-SLP

Student: Zachary Brugger, fifth grade

See "Bored Bobby" to learn more about Ryan and Zachary.

Meditation Matt (Page 112)

Ginny Thompson, MS, CCC,-SLP
See "Brakester" to learn more about Ginny.

Student: D., elementary school student

Miss Turn Taker (Page 45)

Mary Deyo, speech language pathologist
Mary loves teaching children about her favorite superhero, Superflex. She was excited to work with students to develop their creative and helpful ideas for new Unthinkable characters. She's so happy that Hannah gets to share Miss Turn Taker with the rest of Social Town!

Student: Hannah Kantor, fourth grade
Hannah chose this character because she thinks a lot of kids have trouble always wanting to be first in line to go places and not being willing to let others take their turn. She says kids should take turns going first and everybody should get a turn, not just Miss Turn Taker.

Mood Keeper (Page 51)

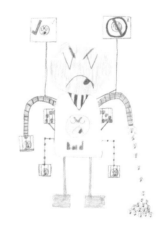

Melissa Da Silva, child and youth worker
Melissa and her colleague, Anne Wiley worked with Dariusz K. in the Program to Assist Social Thinking for the past four years. Dariusz is an especially talented boy who sometimes lets his mood get the best of him. One day he realized he needed a villain that targeted his difficulty, which is keeping his mood bad. Mood Keeper was born! Since then, Dariusz created a poster-size Mood Keeper to help other children in the program and a pocket-size Mood Keeper for himself to help get through the day. Dariusz has improved tremendously and they're extremely proud of him at P.A.S.T.

Student: Dariusz K., sixth grade

Mr. Whoemeye (Page 108)

Elizabeth J. Davis, speech language pathologist
See "The Bad Exampler" to learn more about Elizabeth.

Student: Frank L. Tompkins, twelfth grade

In the past, Frank says he's been unsure of who he is and wants to be. He picked this Unthinkable because it explains a lot about his life and what has happened in his past. Superflex beats this Unthinkable by reminding him that he is Frank and can be himself.

Munchie Munchie (Page 58)

Ryan Hendrix, MS, CCC-SLP

Student: Zachary Brugger, fifth grade

See "Bored Bobby" to learn more about Ryan and Zachary.

Negasorus Nix (Page 67)

Abigail Jaffe, MA, CCC-SLP

Abigail is a speech language pathologist and co-founder of Communication Therapy Associates. One of her middle school Social Thinking groups decided to enter the contest as a fun way to help younger children. Along the way they realized that although Superflex is a program for younger children, teens and adults have to fight many of the same Unthinkables.

Students: Spencer Laffond, Sam Falcetti, and Ryan Walsh

Negative Future Charge (Page 107)

Dominic Petillo, behavioral specialist

Dominic has been using Superflex with his students for three years. He's found it helpful for his students to create their own Unthinkables to address their particular behavioral needs. Negative Future Charge was created by a very insightful student who recognized that he worries too much about negative things happening in the future. Through DBT mindfulness exercises, students have learned to slow down and focus on what people can control — the present.

Student: S.S.

Negative Nick (Page 102)

Kelly Bleckley, MA, CCC-SLP, social cognitive therapist

Kelly is a social cognitive therapist who has been a part of the Social Thinking-Stevens Creek team for two-and-a-half years. This Unthinkable was created for a specific student who had difficulty thinking of anything positive to say. His thoughts would naturally go toward focusing on the negative. Having this as an Unthinkable to beat created motivation to start to think and say more positive things.

Nancy Weston, LFMT

Nancy is a licensed marriage family therapist who works for Social Thinking-Stevens Creek. As Kelly described, Negative Nick was inspired by one of their clients who struggled with viewing new situations, meeting new people, and being offered new opportunities because of his negative perspective. The challenge was how to defeat Negative Nick with Superflex strategies.

Student: D.H.I., fourth grade

D. has been attending Teach Social since the summer before third grade. Negative Nick is the Unthinkable that often shows up in his life. D. wants this Unthinkable to disappear — and works hard to make that happen.

Noodle Dude (Page 45)

Ryan Hendrix, MS, CCC-SLP

See "Bored Bobby" to learn more about Ryan.

Nosey Rosey (Page 80)

Kristy Chopp, special education teacher

Kristy is from Oshkosh, Wisconsin. She became a member of Social Town two years ago. She created Nosey Rosey to help students understand that putting their mind and ears into other people's business makes people feel uncomfortable. Nosey Rosey proved to be simple, direct, and effective!

Past Willy (Page 52)

Dominic Petillo, behavioral specialist

Past Willy is an Unthinkable created by an insightful student who recognized that the student frequently brings problems from home or recess into the classroom (or vice versa). Dominic has been able to successfully use this character and intervention with numerous students. He particularly likes this Unthinkable because he invades us all at one point or another and can be quite pesky!

Perfect Patty (Page 82)

Reneé Attaway, speech language pathologist and Social Thinking therapist at The Parish School

Renee named this Unthinkable in response to a student telling her he didn't have any other Unthinkables and he was so worried that it meant he wasn't perfect at something. He also couldn't do his homework because it took forever… and he always had to make perfect grades! Renee thinks this sounds like so many of us! Her students have really identified with this Unthinkable. Contact her at renee.attaway@gmail.com with more questions or look up the Parish School at www.parishschool.org.

Perfect Pete (Page 81)

Melanie Mosher, SLPA

Melanie is a speech language therapist with her own company called Bright Bird Therapy Services. The Unthinkables that she created stemmed from different needs of students in a group that came from unexpected behaviors that the students were participating in. Volume Volumizer in particular was something her entire program used because the kids had trouble staying quiet. Melanie is almost finished with her Masters degree, focusing on autism. She's been in the field for eleven years.

Tim Huesken, illustrator

Tim works for GameHouse Canada as a senior artist. He has his own website, http://shinybluerobot.com, where all of his work is displayed.

Picky Peater (Page 59)

Judy Sotelo, speech language pathologist

Student: J.Q.K., fourth grade
Judith works as a speech language pathologist at Pediatric Speech and Language Specialists in Scottsdale, Arizona. In the fall of 2011, one of the children in a social language group submitted an entry with his new Unthinkable Picky Peater. It was his idea based on his own difficulty with eating. He designed it and Judy just helped facilitate his entry. She describes J. as an awesome ten year old who loves sports. He loves to participate and be a spectator. She says that he can tell you just about anything you might need to know about baseball or basketball, and his favorite teams are the New England Patriots and any team from The University of Connecticut. He shares this passion with his dad and he's been all over the country watching amazing games! Judy says to give J. all the credit for this entry!

Please Activate Waiting System (P.A.W.S.) (Page 113)

Jenny Moss, former special education teacher, current PhD student

Student: Annie Moss, second grade
See "Justice Buster" to learn more about Jenny and Annie.

Potty Mouth Pete (Page 91)

Claudia Weiss, LCSW
Claudia has extensive experience in facilitating children's groups, giving workshops, and developing curriculum for social skills. She's the co-creator of Too Much, Too Little, Just Right and Too Close, Too Far, Just Right, which are games used nationally to address tone of voice and personal space. She has a private practice in Malboro, New Jersey.

Sandra Singer, PhD
Sandra is a school psychologist who has written articles on counseling and character education. She's the co-creator of the therapeutic games Too Much, Too Little, Just Right and Too Close, Too Far, Just Right. She's an adjunct assistant professor at Rider University with a private practice in Malboro, New Jersey.

Lois Feigenbaum, LCSW

Lois has worked with children and families for over 25 years. She has extensive experience in leading groups for children and providing professional workshops on social skills. She is the co-creator of Too Much, Too Little, Just Right, and Too Close, Too Far, Just Right. She has a private practice in South Orange, New Jersey.

Matilda Mato, MFA

Matilda is a British-born artist and New Jersey certified K–12 art teacher. Matilda earned her BFA in drawing and painting from Ohio State University and her master's in fine arts education from Kean University. She currently teaches elementary art while earning a second master's in supervision and administration.

Prickly Pete the Porcupine (Page 53)

Mark Lee, student, age 24

Mark says he had long periods of time where he was unhappy with his situation and would often be in an overly rash and bad mood around others. Even in social settings he says he would tend to sit on his own and get annoyed and angry at people who were friendly enough to approach him (though most people took one look at him and thought, "Boy, he doesn't seem too friendly"). Many people who did approach him left thinking, "I'm sorry I asked."

Professorus Wrecks (Page 106)

Alana Fichtelberg, MA, CCC-SLP

Alana has been a speech language pathologist for 17 years. As a Social Town citizen for two years, she helps citizens aged 5 to 16 use their Superflex powers. Many students use "professorial" talk, with words that peers don't understand or use. This causes others to have weird thoughts about them. Professorus Wrecks can be defeated by using Superflex powers.

Student: Jake Micheletti, third grade

Jake is a nine-year-old aspiring rock star who loves to play the drums, video games, ride his bike, and eat out. He's working on not allowing Professorus Wrecks to come out by using words that kids his age say.

Queen of Wacky Questions (Page 38)

Alana Fichtelberg, MA, CCC-SLP

Alana (see "Professorus Wrecks") says students ask too many questions, questions they know the answers to, or unimportant/irrelevant questions, and then others have weird thoughts about them. Superflex needs to calm down Queen of Wacky Questions.

Student: Shawn Kavanaugh, sixth grade

Shawn is a 12-year-old future movie critic. He loves video games and going to the movies. He's working on holding back Queen of Wacky Questions so that there's time to play the game during a session and working on asking questions that are important and related to the topic.

Rainbow Girl (Page 111)

Nicole Aronowitz, speech language pathologist
Nathan Dybvig, special education teacher

Student: Frances H. Zercher, eighth grade

Rainstorm (Page 52)

Student: Reid S., fourth grade

Reid attends classes at Teach Social. He came up with the Unthinkable Rainstorm to help him deal with issues that cloud his mind and follow him around.

Refuso (Page 68)

Ginny Thompson, MS, CCC-SLP

See "Brakester" to learn more about Ginny.

Student: D., elementary school student

Rule Police (Page 56)

Todd Markham, school psychologist

Todd is a nationally certified school psychologist at Pine Grove School in Avon, Connecticut. He became a member of Social Town in the role of providing direct social skill instruction to small groups of elementary school students. He takes great pride in helping students defeat the Team of Unthinkables.

Ruler Rod (Page 92)

Kelly Bleckley, MA, CCC-SLP

Kelly's journey with Social Thinking started in graduate school while attending San Jose State University. She's a speech language pathologist who completed her student externship at the Social Thinking-Stevens Creek clinic, studying under Pamela Crooke, Ryan Hendrix, and Kari Palmer. Ruler Rod emerged onto the scene during her externship while she was working with Ryan. The group they were working with continued to correct each other, point out any type of mistake, and stay strictly to the exact rules, especially while playing games. (See "Negative Nick" to learn more about Kelly.)

Ryan Hendrix, MS, CCC-SLP
See "Bored Bobby" to learn more about Ryan.

Shurman Shirker (Page 84)

Becky Fukuda, paraeducator
See "Attention Eater" to learn more about Becky.

Space Raptor (Page 115)

Allison Ramirez, speech language pathologist
Allison is a speech language pathologist at Fairview Elementary, Denver Public Schools. Her student Alexus was the inspiration for Space Raptor and Allison says that his talent and creativity drove this project.

Student: Alexus D. Dominguez, fourth grade
Alexus created Space Raptor to be Superflex's sidekick to help conquer the team of Unthinkables. A video and the Team of Unthinkables guided his creation of Space Raptor. He wanted students across the nation to see Space Raptor and believe they can overcome any obstacles with strength, flexibility, and confidence. Ms. Alli introduced him to Social Thinking, encouraged him to enter the contest, and helped him through this process. He hopes Space Raptor and the Team of Unthinkables will help students as Superflex has helped him.

ABOUT THE CONTRIBUTORS

Space Respecter (Page 114)

Deanna Amborn, speech language pathologist
Deanna has worked for St. Paul public schools in a K–6 elementary school setting for 16 years.

Student: Ella Amborn, preschool
Ella is the four-and-a-half year old daughter of Deanna and a successful user and creator of Thinkables and Unthinkables.

Space Squid (Page 97)

Marsha B. Schoene-Langohr, teacher
Student: Russell C., third grade
See "Big Bubble Bob" to learn more about Marsha and Russell.

Stick to Me Sam (Page 61)

Mary Hollis Keiger
Mary is a Social Skills director at Forsyth Country Day School in North Carolina. She has over 20 years of experience working with children with autism as well as children with other social difficulties. Currently, Mary leads social skills groups for children in preschool to young adults.

Sticky Fingers (Page 89)

Deborah Finkelstein, NCC, LCPC
See "Garbage Can Crew" to learn more about Deborah.

Storyteller (Page 95)

Lisa Schwoerke, school psychologist
Lisa works as a school psychologist at Roaring Brook Elementary School. She enjoys working with groups of children and helping them to understand their own sets of strengths.

Students: Mya K. and Joshua Z.
Mya describes herself as a student with an interest in learning. The Thinkables and Unthinkables caught her attention and she's been interested ever since. She hopes that one day, our world will be Superflex, who knows how to control emotions.

Joshua says he developed this Unthinkable because sometimes he lies. Superflex has to defeat Storyteller throughout the day so then he doesn't lie.

Sunny Sun (Page 120)

Deanna Amborn, speech language pathologist

Student: Ella Amborn, preschool
See "Space Respecter" to learn more about Deanna and Ella.

Talks Too Much Tess (Page 101)

Sandra Singer, PhD
Claudia Weiss, LCSW
Lois Feigenbaum, LCSW
Matilda Mato, MFA
See "Potty Mouth Pete" to learn more about Sandra, Claudia, Lois, and Matilda.

Tattle Taylor (Page 93)

Lisa Carter, EdS, NCSP
See "Antsy Nancy" to learn more about Lisa.

The Bad Exampler (Page 103)

Elizabeth J. Davis, speech language pathologist
Elizabeth works at Spurwink Services' Brunswick Staff Intensive Program. She lives in Social Town, Maine where they have lots of visits from new Unthinkables. She has a feeling that some of these Unthinkables travel from town to town. She wants to make sure that others are on the lookout for these Unthinkables and know how to defeat them if they come in contact with them!

Student: Amanda Queening, eleventh grade
Amanda developed the Unthinkable The Bad Exampler because many of her idols are singers, rappers, and movie stars. Amanda says some of these people make bad choices and don't think before they act, and she tried to be like them. She says that she made some bad choices and now wants her role models to be good influences.

ABOUT THE CONTRIBUTORS
CHAPTER 6 © 2012 SOCIAL THINKING PUBLISHING

The Confuser (Page 63)

Kathie Kennelly, PhD
Kathie holds an MA and PhD in speech language pathology from the University of Illinois and has practiced in the field for 30+ years. She first became acquainted with Social Town three years ago. Superflex has successfully assisted her students in fighting invasions of the Unthinkables ever since!

The Enforcer (Page 54)

Audra Jensen, MEd, BCBA, director of Autism Behavioral Consulting

Debbie McCord, BA, BCaBA, program manager, illustrator of The Enforcer
See "Int-Erupter" to learn more about Audra and Debbie.

The Junkanator (Page 59)

Sylvia Granet, parent
Sylvia is the author and mom who coordinated mailing materials.

Donna Wexler, speech language pathologist
Donna introduced Emily to the Social Town curriculum back in 2008.

Nicole Granet, 17 years old
Nicole is Emily's older sister who helped Emily with the graphics program.

Student: Emily Granet, eighth grade
Emily lives in Boca Raton, Florida and adores Pokémon and animals! Born with intestinal problems, Emily didn't eat by mouth for the first three years of her life. She had a feeding tube and only learned to eat by mouth after leaving home twice to attend therapeutic feeding programs. For most of her young life, eating was very difficult and she had trouble keeping weight on. Her doctors insisted she eat fattening foods to gain weight. At puberty, the junky foods began taking their toll on her weight and she had to relearn to eat healthier foods. With self-determination, she has battled The Junkanator and wishes to inspire other kids to do the

same. Emily has been greatly inspired by Superflex and learned so much from the Unthinkables. She is so proud to join other authors in this publication of additional Unthinkables that will help children battle their weaknesses.

The Whiner (Page 41)

Deborah Finkelstein, NCC, LCPC
See "Garbage Can Crew" to learn more about Deborah.

Thin Flin (Page 64)

Andrea Bukovinszky, school psychologist

Judy Hale, speech language pathologist
Andrea and Judy teach a weekly Lunch Bunch for Social Thinking at Golden School in Placentia, California. They love Superflex and helping students to be able to think flexibly to solve problems. Andrea loves elephants and Judy collects flamingos.

Student: Kevin Mabry, fourth grade
Kevin is nine years old and goes to school at Golden School in Placentia. He plays soccer and likes to watch basketball. He has one older sister and one younger brother. They have three cats and two dogs. His favorite subject in school is geology.

T.S. (Thumbsucker) (Page 96)

Melanie Mosher, SLPA

Tim Huesken, illustrator
See "Perfect Pete" to learn more about Melanie and Tim.

Tim Taskstick-Able (Page 118)

Deanna Amborn, speech language pathologist

Student: Ella Amborn, preschool
See "Space Respecter" to learn more about Deanna and Ella.

Time Keeper (Page 56)

Ginny Thompson, MS, CCC-SLP
See "Brakester" to learn more about Ginny.

Student: Sadie V., second grade

Time Racer (Page 46)

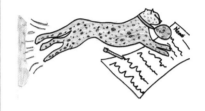

Chris Paulson, speech language pathologist
Chris says that last spring, they were getting ready to take comprehensive reading and math tests when a third grade teacher talked about students who worked too fast and didn't produce quality work. Their brain sensor alarm sounded! They called on their flexible brains to design their Unthinkable Time Racer.

Students: Emily Walsh, Mateusz Kukla, and Andy B.

Tiny Teacher (Page 57)

Rebecca L. Hack, K-2 special education teacher

Tiffani Schmitt, school social worker
See "Inter-Ruptor" to learn more about Rebecca and Tiffani.

Toxicore (Page 79)

Christa Jachym, special education teacher
Christa teaches at the Benhaven Learning Center in Wallingford, Connecticut where she works with students of various social abilities. They use and embed Social Thinking strategies and the Superflex curriculum throughout our day. Her students are extremely innovative and enjoy the challenge of developing their ideas to share with others.

Student: Matthew Blecker, seventh grade

Volume Volumizer (Page 98)

Melanie Mosher, SLPA
Tim Huesken, illustrator
See "Perfect Pete" to learn more about Melanie and Tim.

Waitin' Mate (Page 85)

Lisa Carter, EdS, NCSP
See "Antsy Nancy" to learn more about Lisa.

Wings (Page 122)

Kristan Shimpi, PhD
Kristan has been working with teachers, parents, and students with ADHD, autism, and learning disabilities since 1995. She's currently an adjunct faculty member at East Carolina University. As a teacher, consultant, and teacher trainer, she helps problem-solve challenging classroom behaviors. She co-developed an academic support skills curriculum at the Duke ADHD Program and has a special interest in students with attention and social difficulties.

Ginny Thompson, MS, CCC-SLP
See "Brakester" to learn more about Ginny.

The Social Town Book Committee

Stephanie Madrigal, Mayor of Social Town
Michelle Garcia Winner, Town Council Member
Pamela Crooke, Town Council Member
Sandra Horwich, Town Council Editor
Elizabeth Blacker, Town Council Book Design and Layout Artist

As this book was being developed, the Mayor asked for a special meeting with members of the Town Council. They met to discuss the best teaching and learning strategies to help Social Town citizens develop more superflexible powers to defeat the growing number of Unthinkables.

As the Mayor's committee talked, they discovered Superflex's Very Cool Five-Step Power Plan. This led them to realize they needed to make some further edits to the descriptions of the Unthinkables and Thinkables that citizens had submitted for this project. As they worked, many of the Unthinkables tried to sabotage the project by creating tremendous powers in the brains of the book committee members.

The Unthinkables that demonstrated their immense powers included Negative Nick, Shurman Shirker, Confusion Carol, Dark Defeatist, Refuso, and Kenny Can't — and those were just some of the ones who got involved. Luckily, the Social Town team of psychologists and counselors came to the aid of the committee with many powerful strategies to defeat the Unthinkables. This gave the committee the power to keep going to present the Very Cool Five-Step Power Plan and to put together this book!

CHAPTER 7

Glossary

This glossary defines some of the commonly used Social Thinking terms you'll find in the descriptions of various Unthinkables and Thinkables in this book. Many other helpful concepts and vocabulary exist and can be found in books from Michelle Garcia Winner, Stephanie Madrigal, or Pam Crooke listed in the Bibliography and also described at www.socialthinking.com.

Glossary

Blue thoughts (blue popsicle sticks) and **red thoughts** (red popsicle sticks): This lesson was developed to teach students about social memory. Many of our students do not realize that what they did yesterday may be remembered tomorrow. To explore this concept we introduce the idea that in general, we have two types of memorable thoughts about people: good thoughts and weird thoughts/uncomfortable thoughts. We teach this visually by using red popsicle sticks to represent behaviors that may cause a person to have an uncomfortable thought about that student, which may lead others to remember that person in a more negative manner. The blue sticks represent behaviors a student may do that cause another person to have a good thought, which possibly leads to a good memory about that student.

This lesson is about teaching students that we think and remember what people do around us. One way to teach this is for an adult teacher or specialist to show a citizen a red popsicle stick or hold one up to his/her head. This encourages the citizen to think about the idea that his/her behavior is leading that adult to have an uncomfortable thought about the student. However, the real power in this lesson is showing a student the many blue stick (good thought) behaviors this student is producing. This helps encourage the student and reinforces that there are many things this student does that adults and fellow citizens feel is expected behavior, behavior that helps keep everyone calm and perhaps even feeling good. It is a mistake for adults to over-emphasize a student's red-stick behaviors. The red-stick lessons are only valuable if the student has been encouraged to celebrate his blue stick behaviors! The citizen is then encouraged to create more behaviors that help produce good thoughts (blue sticks).

For more information on the complexity of teaching this lesson, please see lesson 12, Good Thoughts/Weird Thoughts, in our *Think Social Curriculum* (Winner, 2005).

Brain filter: A fun imaginary way to think about citizens' brains having a screen or a filter that keeps in unexpected or mean thoughts. Expected and friendly thoughts pass through the filter so citizens can say them aloud.

Fidget: A small item that citizens can hold in their hands or touch to keep their hands busy. They can use the fidget to help them focus or keep their hands to themselves. A fidget works best when it's out of sight (held under the desk or table) so it doesn't become a distraction.

Lock box: An imaginary box in a person's brain that helps citizens think about the words they're using around people. If a person realizes that the words she or he is about to use may be bossy, unfriendly, or sound like the Rule Police, the person can imagine taking those words and putting them in the box with the lock on tight to keep from saying them aloud.

Mind map: A visual design that can be created on paper or by using software programs or apps to organize thoughts and ideas around a topic or main idea.

One-arm rule: A measurement for thinking about how close a person should be to other people — about one arm's length. This rule can be a good start to figuring out physical space.

People file: A way to think about gathering information that a citizen learns about others. These pretend files are created when citizens meet new people and are reopened when citizens are around others they know. Citizens then can "open" their people file to remember something about the person they're talking to and show the person that they're thinking about him or her.

Social Behavior Map: A visual tool to demonstrate that in a specific situation, the manner in which a person is treated by others depends in large part on how that person has made others feel based on using expected or unexpected behaviors. Students are encouraged to explore

1. Whether their behaviors are expected or unexpected for the situation.
2. How people feel about the student based on the behaviors produced.
3. How people react to the student based on how they feel about the student.
4. How students feel about themselves as a result of how they are treated when people react to their behavioral response.

Social Behavior Mapping is explained further, and in different ways, in three of our books:

1. *Thinking About YOU Thinking About ME* (Winner, 2007); a chapter is dedicated to SBM.
2. *Social Behavior Mapping* (Winner, 2007); this book provides many examples of completed SBM charts as well as provides basic instructions and templates.

3. *Socially Curious and Curiously Social* (Winner and Crooke, 2009); a graphic novel to encourage fifth to ninth grade students to explore this social emotional chain reaction.

Social wonder: Asking questions that show interest in the thoughts, activities, or preferences of another person. This shows you are trying to be friendly as well as helps you learn more about others' interests.

Thought journal: This could be a few pieces of paper or a blank journal book where citizens write down thoughts or ideas that they're not able to share because they were off topic or because sharing would have interrupted someone who was talking or taken the teacher away from the lesson plan.

World wonder: Asking questions about facts that are only interesting to the person asking the question. People may feel you are not interested in them when you ask too many questions of this type.

Worry journal: A piece of paper or a book where citizens can write down a worry they have in their brain. Writing down the worry may help the citizen let go of it.

CHAPTER 8
Bibliography

This Bibliography includes books you can use to learn more about Superflex, Social Thinking, and superflexible strategies students can use to defeat Unthinkables. See www.socialthinking.com for additional resources.

Briers, S. (2009). *Brilliant Cognitive Behavioural Therapy: How to Use CBT to Improve Your Mind and Your Life*. Upper Saddle River, NJ: Prentice Hall.

Buron, K. and Curtis, M. (2004). *The Incredible 5-Point Scale*. Shawnee Mission, KS: Autism Asperger Publishing Company.

Crooke, P. and Winner, M. (2011). *Social Fortune or Social Fate*. San Jose, CA: Social Thinking Publishing.

Kuypers, L. (2011). *The Zones of Regulation: A Curriculum Designed to Foster Self-Regulation and Emotional Control*. San Jose, CA: Social Thinking Publishing.

Madrigal, S. (2008). *Superflex® Takes on Rock Brain and the Team of Unthinkables*. San Jose, CA: Social Thinking Publishing.

Madrigal, S. and Winner, M. (2008). *Superflex®…A Superhero Social Thinking Curriculum*. San Jose, CA: Social Thinking Publishing.

Madrigal, S. and Winner, M. (2009). *Superflex® Takes On Glassman and the Team of Unthinkables*. San Jose, CA: Social Thinking Publishing.

Madrigal, S. and Winner, M. (2012*). Superflex® Takes on Brain Eater and the Team of Unthinkables*. San Jose, CA: Social Thinking Publishing.

Reaven, J., et al. (2011). *Facing Your Fears: Group Therapy for Managing Anxiety in Children with High-Functioning Autism Spectrum Disorders*. Baltimore: Brookes Publishing.

Winner, M. editor. (2007). *Social Behavior Mapping: Connecting Behavior, Emotions and Consequences Across the Day*. San Jose, CA: Social Thinking Publishing.

Winner, M. and Crooke, P. (2008). *You Are a Social Detective!* San Jose, CA: Social Thinking Publishing.

Winner, M. and Crooke, P. (2011). *Socially Curious and Curiously Social: A Social Thinking Guidebook for Bright Teens and Young Adults*. San Jose, CA: Social Thinking Publishing.

BIBLIOGRAPHY

About the Editors and Social Thinking Publishing

Stephanie Madrigal

Stephanie Madrigal, MS, CCC-SLP is a speech language pathologist who co-developed the Superflex teaching series with Michelle. She received her BA and MA from San Jose State University and worked at the Social Thinking Center for many years. Stephanie now resides in Watsonville, California, and is part of Growing Social, a program to teach children with social learning challenges within an organic farm environment.

A creative therapist who infuses humor and fun into teaching, Stephanie co-authored with Winner, *Superflex... A Superhero Social Thinking Curriculum* (2007) and three other related Superflex comic books.

Michelle Garcia Winner

Michelle Garcia Winner, MA, CCC-SLP is a speech language pathologist who specializes in the treatment of students with social cognitive deficits at the Social Thinking Center, her clinic in San Jose, California. She coined the term "Social Thinking®" in the mid-1990s and created the Social Thinking framework that today includes information, vocabulary, curriculum, and strategies that help individuals with social learning challenges.

Michelle works with clients ranging from children to adults, consults with families and schools, and travels internationally giving presentations on all aspects of Social Thinking. She has written or co-authored more than 20 books on the framework, all of which are published through Social Thinking Publishing. In 2008, she was awarded a Certificate of Special Congressional Recognition for developing her treatment approach. Her work led GreatSchools.org, a prominent national nonprofit organization, to call Michelle, "...the leading expert in the field of social skills."

Pamela Crooke

Pamela J. Crooke, PhD is a speech language pathologist and is the Director of Research and Clinical Operations and Senior therapist at the Social Thinking Center in San Jose, CA. She maintains an active caseload of children, teens, and adults, conducts Dynamic Assessments, and consults with school programs. She has co-authored, with Winner, four award-winning books related to Social Thinking: *Socially Curious and Curiously Social, You Are a Social Detective, Social Fortune or Social Fate,* and *Social Thinking at Work: Why Should I Care?*

Pam is a prolific writer and sought-after international speaker. Her research-based article documenting the effectiveness of using the Social Thinking vocabulary, "Brief report: Measuring the Effectiveness of Teaching Social Thinking to Children with Asperger Syndrome (AS) and High Functioning Autism (HFA), (Crooke, Hendrix, & Rachman, 2008), was published in the *Journal of Autism and Developmental Disorders.*

About Social Thinking Publishing

The team at Social Thinking Publishing, led by Michelle Garcia Winner, is dedicated to publishing quality books and products, and hosting conferences around the world that explore and broaden our ideas of what it means to think social, be social, and teach social thinking and related social skills. Today, the company reaches tens of thousands of parents and professionals annually around the globe through its dynamic conferences and release of thought-provoking books and products written by Winner and Crooke as well as by innovative professionals using the Social Thinking framework. Learn more at www.socialthinking.com.

Check out our fun and informative conference day about teaching the Superflex curriculum: "Superflex & Friends Take on Social Emotional Learning and The Common Core Standards" presented in locations across the U.S.

Core Books About the Social Thinking Model & Related Teaching Strategies

Inside Out: What Makes a Person with Social Cognitive Deficits Tick?
By Michelle Garcia Winner

For professionals and parents to use with all ages!

The starting place to learn about the ILAUGH Model upon which Social Thinking is based. Discusses the direct connection between social thinking and academic problems such as reading comprehension and written expression, and helps readers pinpoint specific challenges in a child or student. Valuable insight on information we expect students to know to become strong learners but that doesn't develop "naturally" in everyone.

Thinking About YOU Thinking About ME, 2nd Edition
By Michelle Garcia Winner

For professionals and parents to use with all ages!

Learn more about social interaction and social awareness! Explains Michelle Garcia Winner's core Social Thinking concepts and treatment methods, with extensive curriculum content on perspective taking as well as assessment using the Social Thinking Dynamic Assessment Protocol®. Age-targeted lesson and activity ideas, templates and handouts included. A precursor to using books like *Superflex, You Are A Social Detective,* and more!

Think Social!
A Social Thinking Curriculum for School-Aged Students, 2nd Edition
By Michelle Garcia Winner

For parents and professionals to use with all ages!

A complement to *Thinking About YOU Thinking About ME,* this is the fundamental Social Thinking curriculum book to help individuals K-12 and into adulthood. The book sequences through eight chapters and 69 lessons that help students explore the basics of working and thinking in a group. Each chapter addresses how to use and interpret language (verbal and nonverbal) to further understand the context of communications.

Social Thinking® books, curriculum, thinksheets, and related products developed by Michelle Garcia Winner and the Social Thinking team

Core Books and Curricula About Social Thinking

Thinking About YOU Thinking About ME, 2nd Edition

Think Social! A Social Thinking Curriculum for School-Age Students

Inside Out: What Makes a Person with Social Cognitive Deficits Tick?

Social Behavior Mapping: Connecting Behavior, Emotions and Consequences Across the Day (also available in Spanish)

Why Teach Social Thinking?

For Early Learners

The Incredible Flexible You™: A Social Thinking Curriculum for the Preschool and Early Elementary Years — co-authored by Ryan Hendrix, Kari Zweber Palmer, and Nancy Tarshis

We Can Make It Better! Stories: A Strategy to Motivate and Engage Young Learners in Social Problem-Solving Through Flexible Stories — by Elizabeth M. Delsandro

For School-Age Children

You Are a Social Detective! — co-authored by Pamela Crooke (also available in French and Spanish)

Superflex®... A Superhero Social Thinking Curriculum — co-authored by Stephanie Madrigal

Superflex® Takes on Rock Brain and the Team of Unthinkables — by Stephanie Madrigal

Superflex® Takes on Brain Eater and the Team of Unthinkables — co-authored by Stephanie Madrigal

Superflex® Takes on Glassman and the Team of Unthinkables — co-authored by Stephanie Madrigal

Superflex® Takes on One-Sided Sid, Un-Wonderer and the Team of Unthinkables — co-authored by Stephanie Madrigal

Social Town Citizens Discover 82 New Unthinkables for Superflex® to Outsmart! — co-edited by Stephanie Madrigal

Superflex® Superdecks: Card Games to Promote Superflexible Social Thinking

Thinkables & Unthinkables Double Deck

I Get It! Building Social Thinking and Reading Comprehension Through Book Chats — by Audra Jensen

Movie Time Social Learning — by Anna Vagin

Should I or Shouldn't I? What Would Others Think?™ A Game to Encourage Social Thinking and Social Problem Solving, Elementary School Edition — by Dominique Baudry

Sticker Strategies: Practical Strategies to Encourage Social Thinking and Organization, 2nd Edition

Thinksheets for Teaching Social Thinking and Related Skills

What Is a Thought? (A Thought Is a Lot) — by Jack Pransky and Amy Kahofer

Whole Body Listening Larry at Home! — by Kristen Wilson and Elizabeth Sautter

Whole Body Listening Larry at School! — by Elizabeth Sautter and Kristen Wilson

The Zones of Regulation®: A Curriculum Designed to Foster Self-Regulation and Emotional Control — by Leah M. Kuypers

For Teens and Young Adults

Should I or Shouldn't I? What Would Others Think?™ A Game to Encourage Social Thinking and Social Problem Solving, Middle School Edition — by Dominique Baudry

Social Fortune or Social Fate: A Social Thinking Graphic Novel Map for Social Quest Seekers — co-authored by Pamela Crooke

Social Thinking at Work: Why Should I Care? A Guidebook for Understanding and Navigating the Social Complexities of the Workplace — co-authored by Pamela Crooke

Social Thinking Thinksheets for Tweens and Teens: Learning to Read in Between the Social Lines

Socially Curious and Curiously Social: A Social Thinking Guidebook for Bright Teens and Young Adults — co-authored by Pamela Crooke

Related Products

Superflex® Takes on the Unthinkables! poster

Superflex's® Very Cool Five-Step Power Plan poster

You Are a Social Detective! interactive CD

Building Blocks of Social Development for Young Children poster

Being Part of a Group poster

Coping with Boring Moments poster

Social Behavior Mapping — Dry Erase Template poster

Social Behavior Mapping — Listening to the Teacher Talk poster

Social Thinking Social Learning Tree poster

Whole Body Listening! poster

The Zones of Regulation® poster

Visit our website for more information on our books and products, free articles on Social Thinking topics, and a listing of Social Thinking conferences across the United States.

www.socialthinking.com